Thomas Mendham

The Wonder Working Water-Mill Displayed

The Mill to Grind Old People Young

Thomas Mendham

The Wonder Working Water-Mill Displayed
The Mill to Grind Old People Young

ISBN/EAN: 9783743401396

Manufactured in Europe, USA, Canada, Australia, Japa

Cover: Foto ©Andreas Hilbeck / pixelio.de

Manufactured and distributed by brebook publishing software (www.brebook.com)

Thomas Mendham

The Wonder Working Water-Mill Displayed

T H E

Wonder Working Water-mill

DISPLAYED.

WITH ITS

Apparatus, Appurtenances, Appendages,
and Operations;

OR, THE

M I L L

TO GRIND OLD PEOPLE YOUNG;

Erected and Practised by the well known DOCTOR, the
learned philanthrophic Friend of

FARMER HODGE.

- However old or maimed don't defpair,
- Come forward, you may find relief when here;
Try but the operations of the mill
You'll own 'twas form'd by more than common fkill.

The RECTOR.

NORWICH:

PRINTED BY CROUSE AND STEVENSON FOR THE AUTHOR,
SOLD BY STEVENSON, AND YARINGTON AND BACON, NORWICH;
AND BY GIVING ORDERS MAY BE HAD OF ANY OTHER
BOOKSELLER IN LONDON OR ELSEWHERE.
PRICE TWO SHILLINGS AND SIXPENCE TO SUBSCRIBERS ONLY,
TO NON-SUBSCRIBERS, THREE SHILLINGS.

MDCC XCI.

DEDICATION.

——————

TO THE

HONEST AND UPRIGHT OF HEART
UNIVERSALLY,

AND TO THOSE WHO ARE POSSESSORS OF

Pure, undefiled Religion especially,

THE FOLLOWING

TRACT

IS MOST DEVOUTLY DEDICATED, BY

THEIR SINCERE SERVANT,

THE AUTHOR.

TREBLE PREFACE;

(OR, THREE SPECIAL PREFACES)

The Firſt by the RECTOR.

BROTHER MORTALS,

I Have both viewed, refided upon (and attended at many operations, indeed I have
at fundry times delivered various Lectures at)
the Wonder Working Mill—I look upon
it to be a moſt ufeful piece of machi-
nery—great numbers have experienced the
unfpeakable advantages derived from the
rules, baths, pedeſtal, works and ways thereof
—I eſteem my learned friend the Doctor,
who fpares neither pains or purſe to do good
—My beſt advice and ready attendance may
be depended upon, fo long as I ſhall be able
to attend, or advife at all—The faid Mill is
fincerely (and without hope or requeſt of
farther emolument here) recommended to
all the fons of Adam; but efpecially to
thofe, who being *grown old*, ſtand moſt in
need of it.

I am, Brethren,
Your devoted and conſtant fervant,
THE RECTOR.

The Second by the DOCTOR.

KINGS, PEERS, PLEBEIANS,
(GENTLEMEN) AND OTHERS.

THE practice of my predeceſſors for ages, and of myſelf for a long ſeries of years, has been the *art of healing*; how far we have been ſuccefsful it does not become me to ſay; let our numerous patients, who are of each ſex, of all degrees, ages, and habits, ſpeak for or cenſure us —my preſent province is to ſay, that for ſome time paſt I have turned my ſtudies, in the healing art, principally to the caſes and cures of thoſe who are properly called *old*. The mill in queſtion has been long erected—the honour has been too liberally imputed to me; it may be true; my fortunes (which are greater than my merits) have been employed for the purpoſe of carrying the operations of the mill into farther effect—I have alſo cheerfully given my attendance, advice, and aſſiſtance for the relief of the diſeaſed; provided medicines, implements, and the like, moſtly *without fee*; this part of my demeanour I learnt from the worthy Rector of our pariſh,

one,

one, who though obliged to live decently, (and well-entitled, if he fo pleafed, to live affluently) on the tithes *the law* of the land gives him, yet, he never burthens his parifh-ioners by exacting the *full tenth*, but gives up his whole time and ftrength to ferve them in prefent and future things, for a decent fufficiency; part of which he diftributes cheerfully to the worthy poor. This, our Rector, who in himfelf feems to me and others, to be a *living body of practical Divinity*, divulged the main of thofe wife and beneficent maxims, by which I learned the conftruction and ufe of this aftonifhing mill —I not only recommend it to all my fellow creatures, who want (as moft do) cure—efpecially to the *old* of every defcription; but I fhall be ready, in concert with my *Rector* and neighbour Hodge (a good natured, plain, plodding farmer, from whofe blunt hints, conceived in humorous language, I confefs to have gathered fome things both pleafing and profitable) I fay, in concert with thofe and others to be met with at the mill, you will find, without fee,

Your willing Phyfician and Friend,

THE DOCTOR.

The Third by *FARMER HODGE.*

LOOK YE, NEIGHBOURS, AND
    EVERY BODY,

YOU may take my word for it if you
    like, and the more to blame you if
you do—come and try, efpecially old hob-
blers, like myfelf, come and try—I fay, and
I will fay any where, I never faw fuch another mill (mind ye) in all the whole courfe
of my life.

Witnefs my hand,

FARMER HODGE.

From my Farm-houfe, called, Highlands
    Farm, December 21, 1790.

THE

Author's General Preface.

Candid Perusers,

A Preface to this work is a compliment you will expect—it is 'one I ought to pay—accept this, and I will be thankful. By a Preface, I conceive, is generally underftood—Firft, fome account of the Author's motive for intruding himfelf in print upon the public—Secondly, A hint of the work itfelf—And, thirdly, An apology for the performance, fo far as the characters of various claffes of men may be involved.

As to motives, I fhould not know what to fay, did not truth dictate—Three months ago I neither thought of a motive to write, or of writing this piece at all, how it came into my mind I know, and if you think the following unadorned, fhort, and artlefs relation, worth a caft of the eye, you will know.

a   I was

(x)

I was defired to attend a perfon of character and confequence on a matter of bufinefs—in obedience to that defire, on Satur-
day the eleventh of December laft I rode for
the Hall, in which that perfon refided—On
approaching it, a thought paffed my mind
concerning " a Mill to grind old People
young," I felt fome force in the idea, but at
that time only reflected, that when young,
I had feen a picture to the like purpofe—I
arrived at the hall, and was foon difmiffed.

On my return, the thought frequently
occurred with additional vigour; " a mill to
grind old people young," it feemed a thought
ftrange and very extraordinary—However, I
did not feel a ftrong defire to banifh it, it dwelt
upon my mind part of the next and the following day; I turned over the fuggeftion,
and foon thought, fomething under that
feemingly whimfical title might be wrote
amufing and inftructive; I began to marfhall
my thoughts, and not long after, at leifure hours, put them on paper—my motives
for fo doing was not to fill my pocket as an
Author, but to try to do *good*; becaufe, I
confider *that* to be my duty as a chriftian,
having

(having received much good) and as a fervant
of that highly favoured community of which
Providence has made me a member.

The work itself has a religious tendency,
though, as to language (in various parts) it
wears a humorous drefs; if that be a fault
it is mine. It would have been extremely
eafy to have put upon it a more folemn, or
(to pleafe fome people) a ftarched garb—
But I was led to drefs it as it appears to the
world, from an apprehenfion, that many
bufy men, would fcarcely touch, much lefs
perufe, a grave toned religious title or tract,
if they found fingle fermonizing, without
fome relief at feafons, by the introductions
of other matters of an inoffenfive, yet fprightly
and cheering caft—to gratify and lead fuch on
from relations harmlefs and pleafing, to truths
experimental and profitable, I am fo far a
conformift, as to have wrote fundry pages,
which the rigid poflee of profeflors (who
are more fond of affected fixed countenances,
fet forms and traditional decorum, than of
experimental fubftances, true purity of heart
and univerfal good will) will hold up as improper, perhaps prophane, frothy, or ridicu-

lous;

lous; to fuch I chufe at prefent only to fay,
here is not a fentence defigned to offend them,
therefore, if they cannot cordially approve,
let them not rafhly condemn—I never
learned or intended to learn their peculiar
creed, and if they are willing to grant me
what they moft eagerly and juftly grafp for
their mother's fons, (that is) liberty to
think lawfully and fpeak freely—as I do
not prefume to cenfure them, they will not,
it is hoped, venture to condemn me.

An apology is effentially neceffary, as it is
confeffed, fome *living characters* (without
previous licence from fuch perfons) are.
brought before the reader's eye—The beft
apology I can make is this—as to individuals,
it may be better not to make applications;
however, no fair one can be made—whoever fairly makes it, to the difadvantage of
any character whatfoever, except fuch general
ones as cry aloud for public, not to fay univerfal avoidance or deteftation, with regard
to refpective bodies of religious men, from
a firm perfuafion, that every fincere worfhip-
per of God has a degree of charity, and
that they all centre in this belief, " We
muft

muſt be prepared for before we can be admitted to Heaven," I have done them the
juſtice that perſuaſion prompted, and have
openly ſaid ſo.

What it is to be ground young is ſufficiently explained at the end of the work.

With the moſt ardent wiſhes for the preſent and future happineſs of all, but eſpecially of the attentive, benevolent, and
chriſtian readers,

I remain,

To the community generally,

and to them particularly,

a willing ſervant,

THOMAS MENDHAM.

Briſton, near Holt, Norfolk,

Feb. 21, 1791.

A Defcription of the Mill itfelf, its Apparatus, Appendages, Perfonages, &c.

The *Father* and Creator.

The *Son* and Redeemer ⎫
The *Holy Ghoft*, Sanctifier, ⎬ Will be eafily underftood
And the Chief Operator, ⎭

The Mill is the true Church of God throughout the earth.

The Meadow—its name defcribes it, i. e. Contemplation.

The River. Reafon—that noble faculty of the foul, called reafon.

The Rivulet—the Grace of God, which brings falvation.

    N. B. Both ftreams run through the true Church, and agitate the main Wheel —that is the Mind of Man.

The Hopper—a ftate of humiliation, which all experience who are truely turned and converted to God—frequently, when nigh to light, they are furrounded by darknefs for a little feafon.

The Two Grinders—fear of deftruction, mixed with hope of deliverance; whoever pafs through thefe and are brought forth right, although before they might be like *old people*, yet, when ground, they become young, or in other words, new creatures.

Concave Mirror—the Penitent's looking-glafs.

Convex Mirror—the Pharifee's looking-glafs.

Plane Mirror—the true Gofpel glafs.

The Spout (or opening)—all pafs through it the moment they become new.

The Pedeftal, or Stool—true heart-felt repentance.

The Beam and Scales—the ftandards or balances of the Sanctuary found in the Scriptures.

Screens—interpofing mercies, placed between the tried and the trials.

The Brufhes—vigilant ftates of mind, by which old dirty practices are done away for ever.

The Wards—in the courfe of the work explain themfelves.

The Baths—baptifms and divers wafhings.

The Rector—the Paftor of the church.

The

The Doctor—a Phyfician of fortune, who gives up his time, and part of his wealth in the caufe of religion.

Hodge—a plain, blunt, honeft farmer, who at firft hefitated about, and rather oppofed the *works of the mill*, but afterwards was willingly ground himfelf.

Hannah, Robert, Audrey, and Sufan, his wife and children, early and fecret con-verts—there are many others of the fame clafs at the mill.

The Young Men and other people—thefe are fincere chriftians, who refide in God's Spiritual Houfe—*the Church*.

The other characters will fpeak for them-felves, and, therefore, need here no ex-planation.

By the Appendages, and country, without the Gate, is meant, the wicked and worldly-minded people, who forget God, and are ftrangers to the privileges real religion affords.

CONTENTS.

CHAPTER V.

CHAPTER VI.

CHAPTER VII.

CHAPTER VIII.

CHAPTER IX.

CHAPTER X.

b

CHAPTER XI.

CHAPTER XII.

Wonder Working Water-mill
DISPLAYED.

CHAPTER I.

A Defcription of the Mill—Its Situation—Appendages—Apparatus—Appurtenances—Attendants, &c. &c.

THIS falutary, medical and reftorative Mill ftands upon a delightful verdant meadow, whofe graffy furface, like a velvet carpet, is ever green; the old inhabitants of the fpot, in ancient days, called it the Meadow of Contemplation. Directly through this meadow runs a bountiful river, called, the River of Reafon; near which flows in conftant foothing murmurs, a clear pellucid rivulet, which often, not always, is received

B   into

into the bosom of the aforesaid river, it is
called the Rivulet Celestial; both the river
and rivulet run through the center of the
mill, and agitate or turn the main wheel,
with its salutary apparatus. Besides the wheel,
the apparatus comprises the hopper, wide
enough to contain more than are willing to
enter it—the two grinders, between which
the patients are tried and turned, or crushed
and maimed, according as they are found prepared or insincere—the spout, or funnel, by
which all those find a passage who endure
the necessary trials—there is in the Mill likewise a seat, stool, or pedestal, which has this
strange property, whoever gets upon it con-
fesses voluntarily the faults and follies of his
past life so long as he sits there—also a beam,
a pair of scales, with sundry weights, by
which the honesty, sincerity and hopeful suf-
ficiency of those who are weighed may be
ascertained—likewise a concave mirror, those
who look into this see their crimes or virtues
magnified—a convex mirror, here, every thing
on the contrary appears less than they are—
there is also a large and noble plane mirror,
or looking-glass, in which all things appear
as they are; moreover there are skreens,

brushes

brufhes, and fundry other things not here to be particularized. The attendants are the Rector, the Doctor, Farmer Hodge, and fundry others, who will appear when the Mill fhall be fet a-going. Thus, thoughtful reader, you have been told of the meadow, the mill, the river, the rivulet, the main wheel, hopper, grinders, fpout, feat, ftool, or pedeftal, beam, fcales and weights, concave mirror, convex ditto, plane ditto, fkreens, brufhes and attendants.

N. B. If you are *old* and want grinding, try this mill, and, that the operations may end happily in your favour, is the hearty wifh of your fervant

The EDITOR.

But, a word of the Appendages before we end the Chapter.

By the appendages are meant, not *technically*, thofe things only that belong to, but thofe alfo that are near the Mill or the Meadow ;· thofe that belong to the Mill comprize fundry feparate wards ; as the wards fet apart for oratory, trial, filence, watching, and other

wards.

wards. There are the bathing rooms alſo,
and a certain fountain belonging to the Mill;
in theſe weak patients are often, if not always,
ſtrengthened, and enabled to act with power
and effect. Thoſe that are near, but do not
belong to this ſpecial precinct, would take a
volume to deſcribe; we ſhall only ſay therefore, juſt beyond the bounds of this place,
there are palaces of falſe pleaſure, decorated
mimic mounts, long avenues, arched gates,
and wide gateways, broad ways, and crooked
paths, where may be ſeen unmeaning pro-
miſers, tinſel grandees, falſe colours, apiſh
modes, ridiculous cuſtoms, gay-coated beg-
gars, fops, fools, fidlers, fortune-hunters,
wine, women, wenches, and a thouſand other
things; and there your ears will be ſaluted,
if not deafened, by prologues, compoſed of
unmeaning compliments, ſilly play fibs,
forged flatteries, rank reproaches, cauſeleſs
careſſes, and petty petitions; and your eyes
may be enchanted or dazzled with ribbons,
laced coats, furbelowed petty ditto, reſin and
cat-gut, wine, bumpers, and veſtals; but,
after the curtain drops, you'll have epilogues
of pallad appetites, pilfered purſes, palſied
limbs, and horrid midnight, morning, or
death-bed

death-bed reflections; from all which, thofe
who pafs through the Mill fincerely fay
GOOD LORD DELIVER US.

CHAPTER II.

*Sundry occurrences and ftrange reports about the
Mill—A few perfons ventured to walk in the
Meadow, they approached the Mill, paffed
through the operations, and became young—A
feaft on the occafion.*

THE fame of the Mill, its ways and
works, foon reached the ears of thofe
who dwelt t'other fide the borders; throngs,
from time to time, approached the fkirts of
the Meadow, but were too fhy to fet foot
upon it; they looked and went their ways,
anon they returned and looked again, at length
feveral ventured to come in at the gate that
lay to the right, and almoft inftantly became
ferious and thoughtful;—they approached the
river Reafon—drank of its falutary ftreams—
the Doctor, with the Rector, who kept a
good

good look out, came together to discourse
with them, and at the very time they were
drinking large draughts of the waters of the
river—the Rector pointed out the Rivulet,
and assured them, though the River water was
good, that of the Rivulet was infinitely better—he added, it is equally *free*—come taste,
and see how good it is—they tasted, and
found the flavour so excellent, that they
earnestly ask for more, and had it; delighted with its comfortable qualities, they
entered the Mill, with the Rector, Doctor and others who dwell on the spot, and
who seeing them come forward went out
to meet them ; the new comers having walked
far, and being weary, sit themselves down on
the seat or pedestal that stands there, just by
the front door, they instantly began to cry
out—you would have been amazed to have
heard them—one and all most bitterly la-
mented;—they acknowledged (to the CHIEF
OPERATOR, *one* who was nigh and heard
them) by what means they became feeble and
old, they expressed the most alarming appre-
hensions, that notwithstanding the fame of the
Mill, they certainly came there to be totally
undone.—The kind Rector took from the
                                    archieves

archives the records of the place—he read,
and affured them, none ever .were undone
who patiently endured the operations of the
Mill—The Doctor brought an emetic, which
(thinking their cafe could not be worfted)
they took, it operated powerfully, fo afterwards he gave them a cordial—they were led
to examine the main wheel, the hopper, the
grinders, the funnel, beam, fcales and weights,
the glaffes, brufhes, and many other things—
upon which they, with one confent, requefted to be received; they were received,
and after pafling through the wards, proving
the ufe of the three mirrors, and after having
their linen well wafhed, and their garments
brufhed, they readily entered the hopper,
paffed between the grinders, and defcended
by the fpout, fo aftonifhingly altered, that,
except their ftature, (which continued the
fame) they appeared as young and as vigorous as thofe who boaft their meridian of
days, or full blown bloom of life; it would
have been highly pleafing to have feen them,
with the Rector, Doctor and dwellers at the
Mill, how they triumphed together (Old
Hodge was not there). It was determined
upon to celebrate the event with a feaft—

the

the feaft was foon prepared, the whole company fit down; they eat fuch things as are
the beft, they drink (but only to comfort,
not to intoxicate) the richeft wine—When
all the young men who had gone through
the operations defired to drop their old and
have new names; new names were given
them, and before the company broke up
one of the new named ftood up and fung
the following fong:

> Could the croud of unbelievers
>   Tell the joys we tafte of here,
> Soon they'd fly from you, deceivers,
>   Join us and our comforts fhare.
> None fo happy, none fo peaceful,
>   None fo cheerfully can fing,
> As we men whofe hearts all graceful,
>   Flame with love unto our King.

CHAPTER

CHAPTER III.

*The Young Men returned to their own country
and families—They were derided and abused
by some—Others, however, withdrew, and
walked in the Meadow.*

THE feaſt being over, theſe new comers
ſaid one to another, let us now return
home to our families and friends, and bring
along with us, when we return, ſuch as are
old and infirm, to embrace, as we have
done, the benefits of the Mill; they, with
hearty thanks to all the operators, eſpecially
to the *Chief,* returned, running, leaping,
walking, ſinging, and telling the wonders
they had found at the Mill; but their countrymen hooted them, and ſaid, they were
outlandiſh people, come from Satan's *dun-
geon, or the* Peake, in Derbyſhire, or elſe
from Lapland, where the world is full of
witches, or ſome where or other; or they
might be blown amongſt them by a whirl-
wind, or dropped like frogs from a cloud, or
water-ſpout.——But ſays the bucks, bloods,
bawds, beauties, bravos, jack-puddings, poſ-

C ture-maſters,

ture-mafters, tumblers, wire-hoppers, mi-
mics, mock-manners, fneerers, grinners,
and fome of the grave men too, get out, or
we'll kick you out ye young monfters, be
gone, here's no abidance for you—Old *Fire-
face*, the landlord of the inn, called the *Jolly Topers*, came, and ftaring upon them, fet
up a horfe-laugh, and fwore by the bottom
of his butts, he had had the honour to keep
the largeft inn in the whole univerfe for up-
wards of three years and three quarters, in
the very heart of the kingdom, where he had
entertained Potentates, Princes, Peers, No-
bles, Ambaffadors, Amblers, and all the
people of the firft rank in the four quarters
of the globe, but he never in all his life before faw or heard of fuch a pack of rabfcal-
lionly, rude, rafcally, ill-looking, ill-fpoken,
intolerable, unfufferable, unbearable fet of
furfeiters as thefe are.—Faugh! fays old Red
Nofe the drawer, the imps fmell of brimftone.
Depend upon it, cries Prim, the pimp of the
Bagnio, by fome fly ftratagem they found a
chink on one fide or the other of ftrumbelow,
or perhaps have crawled out of the bottom-
lefs pit to infect us.—At the inftant up comes
Lawrence Lafh, the driver of the ftage coach

from

from afar; and he, after hearing a part of the
charming converfation, and looking fteadfaftly
at the ftrangers, leeringly protefted, he had
travelled over all the world (partly) and his
coach, the beft any road could boaft of, had
tranfported creatures of all nations and languages, but (fays he) I fwear, on the credit
of my old horfe Quitter, I never faw fuch a
pack of paltroons as thefe are in my life, except once when my flying machine was waf-
ted over land and fea with a parcel of paffen-
gers to Jerufalem; there indeed I did fee
fome fuch monfters—and though thefe have
loft their (long beards, or) chin-geers, depend
upon it they are Jews; Ay, ay, fays Fire-face,
Red-nofe, Pimp, &c. &c. Mr. Lafh, you
are all o' the right on't—We dare fwear they
are all rank Jews, and are come here to clip,
ftew, and fweat all our guineas, and take us
in again for the ninepences and fixpences;
away with thefe Solomons, Mofes', Aarons,
and Jacobs from the face of the earth; lay
hold of them there, duck them, drown
them—At that turbulent time, an old woman, with halfpenny puddings and penny
pies, worn down in the fervice of the place,
ftood by, and fhe began to whine out, hold!

C 2   hold!

hold! fons, you are all in the wrong, they
are neither Jews nor Chriftians, ye fools you;
why, I have in my early days been in Tur-
key, through Holland and China, and fo I
can tell you what they are, why they are
Hottentots' or elfe Cherokees, the one or
t'other of them—Why you lying old bag-
gage, fays Pimp, that can't be, for they have
not black fkins—Good lack a day, child, fays
the old wench, I did not mind their fkins;
a buftle amongft themfelves foon enfued, and
in the confufion the men made their efcape,
and each, after agreeing at a fixed time to
meet at the Mill, returned to his own family.

But can you believe it! they feemed as
ftrange to their relations as they did to their
countrymen—thefe were fure, (they faid)
they were not the fame creatures they ufed
to be, their geftures, looks, lives, language,
tempers, in fhort, in every thing they were fo
altered that they neither could nor would
bear with them; to be fo often talking about
the meadow, the mill, the river, rivulet,
fountain, ftool of repentance, wards, watch-
ings, and a heap of outlanding gibberifh;
and then to diflike all their old favourite ways,

to

to fhun the mounts, gates, broad road, (the eafieft way in the world to walk in) to defpife the cuftoms of the country, and above all to teftify againft thofe honeft fine fellows. Fire-face, Red-nofe, Prim Pimp, Lafh, the driver, and all the fine folks of the place, and laftly, to raife a report that moft of the people of that place were grown old, deformed, crippled, or enfeebled, and therefore wanted grinding, was intolerable, infufferable, provoking, inflaming, difmally dangerous, and not to be fuffered; therefore, with one confent they laid hold of the young men, and drove them away out of the place.

Soon as they were left, they affembled together and refolved to return to the mill, and to beg of the Rector and Doctor to let them abide there; and at the fame time to declare, that for food and raiment they would not long be chargeable, for that as foon as the hurly burly was over they would go into the country by day, and endeavour to get labour for their hands.—That they would be faithful to their employers, ftand their hours, earn their wages, and each evening come back and affift in grinding, if they might but be permitted to lodge at the mill; their request

queſt was ſoon gratified, they took up their lodging there, and for ſome time remained in peace with the Rector, Doctor, Aſſiſtants, and ſometimes with old Hodge, who ſuffered them to viſit his farm-houſe, and as he thought them good fellows, he ſet on two or three of them to work at his farm.

In a ſhort time, the remainder, early in a morning, walked into the country, and aſked for employment, being now unknown, ſome inſtantly got into buſineſs, ſo did the reſt ſometime after; thus all were got to work, and able to earn enough for themſelves in their moderate way of living, and found ſomething to ſpare; this overplus the young men always gave to the *worthy* poor, eſpecially to the ſick, the blind, widows, fatherleſs children, and orphans; and they thought and found in the end, what they gave in charity was like ſeed ſown on a good ſoil, for it brought a very large encreaſe—moreover, wherever they came they would talk, when proper occaſion offered, of the meadow, the wonderful mill, the Rector, the Doctor, and the peaceable, happy young people who dwelt on the ſpot, ſo that many looked upon them and wondered; ſome

thought

thought them mad, fome drunk; fome faid
they were dreadful deceivers, for that there
was no fuch mill under the fun; 'twas a
cheat from top to bottom, nor were there
any people fo happy upon earth. Others
confidered the matter more attentively, and
watching the ways of thefe men, and obferving they appeared happy, and were found
faithful and honeft, began to think there
muft be fomething more than common in the
matter; Mark! the laft had juft before (to
get out of the noife of their place) withdrew
in the twilight, and took a turn or two in
the pleafant meadow, but had never gone fo
far as the mill, &c.

CHAPTER

CHAPTER IV.

Some account of Lord Lothario—His manner of life—The consequences—His hiring Joseph, one of the young men from the mill—And his going with him to the meadow, the mill it-self, &c.

AMONGST the laſt was a Noble Peer, heretofore called Lord Lothario, who happened to employ one of theſe young men in the capacity of ſuperintendant, over his numerous domeſtics, and who, at his leiſure hours, (which were but few) had not only obſerved ſomething ſingular in the fellow (as he called him) but led by curioſity he had queſtioned him—at length he repoſed great *truſt* in him, for he found *Joseph* (that was his name) took care to keep his inferior ſervants at their employments; and not only ſo, but he rebuked them for and kept them from extravagance, gluttony, and drunken-neſs, ſo, that his eſtate, which before was weak, and about to be put out to nurſe, began to grow ſtrong; and this ſo far drew

his

his condefcenfion and regard, that he frequently fpoke to Jofeph; and Jofeph taking
now and then an opportunity to drop a
word about the wonders of the mill—the
Chief Operator there—the meadow, the Doctor, the Rector, his companions, Farmer
Hodge and his family, &c. One day, I'll
tell you what, Joe, fays Lothario, I have
company coming to dinner, and am engaged
at a rout about midnight; but if in the
evening you'll ftop in your way home at the
right gate of your meadow (as you call it)
I'll come to you there in difguife, and if
you o'nt difcover me, I'll pafs for one of your
people, and flip with you into the mill, only
to take a peep at her and your gentry there;
I fhall be glad of that, fays Jofeph, my Lord,
and if your Lordfhip will forgive me, I wifh
you may be prevailed upon to try the works
of the wheels, and that you may find as
much benefit as I have done—Thank ye, Joe,
but hum!—Joe?—My Lord?—I fuppofe one
can have a little entertainment there, have you
any good wine at the mill? the beft under
Heaven, my Lord, but it is not fuch as
your Lordfhip ufually drinks;—Well, well,
but are there any pretty girls there, Jofeph;

D   you'll

you'll excufe me, but I am very fond of the
fair-fex, though, to tell you the truth, I can
do little more than talk with them—Pretty
girls, my Lord, yes, a few of the youngeft,
fineft, and moft beautiful girls in the world,
and yet, pardon my bluntnefs and freedom,
my Lord, I firmly believe not a lewd one
amongft them—The deuce lye ye, Joe, exclaimed Lothario, if they are young, fine, and
beautiful, they are not all veftals; however,
go at eve to the gate, and depend upon it you
fhall have me for a companion.

At evening, as ufual, Jofeph returned in
his way to the mill, he entered the meadow
at the gate, and fat down to wait for Lothario. In the leifure half hour, as he feldom
was idle, Jofeph, ever cheerful, folaced himfelf by finging a fong, and when we have
drawn the outlines of the Peer's charaĉter,
perhaps you may hear it.

Lothario had the fortune (or misfortune,
which ever it is, for the learned are divided in
their opinion on the fubjeĉt) foon after he
was born, to be entitled, by the demife of
the Peer, his father, and death of the Dow-
ager, his mother, to a diftinguifhed title and
a princely fortune, to wit, a landed eftate of
about

about 6000l. a year, and 100,000l. in the funds; during his minority, tho' frequently indulged, yet bridled in part by preceptors, tutors, guardians, and others, he could not (as he uſed to exprefs it) have ſufficient el- bow room; to be ſure, he was half compel- led to learn ſomething, and being of a quick turn of mind, was led up, not only to a to- lerable but to a good education; moreover, he was ſoon accompliſhed in the faſhionable fancies of dancing, fencing, riding the great horſe; and anon, he got himſelf accompliſh- ed in the fine arts of hunting, racing, gamb- ling, wagering, ſwearing, banqueting, and wenching; he had indeed before eighteen an- ticipated his fortune (as ſnug as he could) about 60,000l. by borrowing at about 50 per cent. of Jews, and laviſhing away the mo- ney upon people called Chriſtians. At the age of twenty-one, (happy æra) a grand feaſt was held at Lothario's hall, to celebrate the happy moment, when he became *his own* maſter—but by the care and attention of the dizzy, untruſty raſcals (ſervants I ſhould have ſaid) about him, it is reported to have coſt him not much more than the trifling ſum of 2500l. Before twenty-two he had

the

the honour to keep a ftud of the beft racers
on the turf, (till others beat them). Before
twenty-three he loft by racing and betting
about fix times more money than the horfes
coft him, tho' true, they coft twice their
worth, he having paid, firft and laft, about
1700l. for them. At twenty-four he fold
them off, and purchafed a dozen very fine
hunters, and pack of fox-hounds, at the
moderate price of 450l. he kept them one
year (huntfman, whippers-in, whippers-out,
fportfmen, fervants, &c. included) fo cheap
'tis fuppofed as at about 580l. Before twenty-
fix he diflocated his neck in a chace, by
plumping at a thick-fet hedge to out-leap
one of his tenants, who happened to be
mounted on a better hunter than his Landlord, and who had the impudence to pufh
the Peer, fuppofing (as he afterwards laugh-
ingly faid) if his Landlord had broke one
neck, he carried another in his jacket pocket;
fome kind brother fox-hunter tumbled off
his fteed, and after fixing his dirty knees
againft Lothario's fhoulders, and his nervous
hands beneath his caput, feemed to be pul-
ling off the Peer's head, as one would pluck
off the head of another fort of *pigeon*; but,

however,

however, he reduced the diflocked part; and his Lordfhip, after fome cluttering in his throat, and involuntary tears from his eyes, began to breathe, and his noddle being fupported whilft he laid on the grafs, his carriage was fent for, he was conveyed to the hall, recovered in two months, and juft before he got about again, one day his valet heard him mutter to the following effect;— If there be any fox-hunting in ——, I wifh my horfes and hounds all there, they have coft me monftrous fums, and nearly broke my neck into the bargain—My Lord, fays, William, his fteady valet, (for his fervants at times dare take liberty to fay any thing to him) I have heard my Grandmother fay, Lucifer never rode a fox-chace in his life, and that if the monies the horfes and hounds coft were given to the pitiable poor it would fill many an empty belly—Empty belly, well, well, mine is empty enough; Will, don't let the Doctor know it, but give me a bumper of brandy, here's a guinea for you.

Will?—My Lord?—I'm fick of hunting, tell Tom Trimmer to-morrow to fend all the horfes to Tatterfall's.—They were fent, and at the fall of the hammer, that Gentle-

man

man knows what they fold for as well as
I do.

N. B. Some of the pack, 'tis faid, got the
murrain, and the others were fold very cheap
indeed to a young Lord who was juft then
about to fet up the fame fort of bufinefs.
When Lothario grew better, and became
cool, his old Steward took courage enough
to remonftrate with him in the *money way*;
creditors by crouds came about the hall, and
began to be infufferably clamorous; tell
them, fays his Lordfhip, I am not at home,
(fibbing being quite fafhionable in fome great
houfes) anon, however, the hall grew too
hot—His Lordfhip faunters out, drops in at
the inn, called, the *Jolly Topers*; Fire-face
all but kifs'd his feet, calls his wife to take
his Grace's orders, but took care firft himfelf to bring into diftant view a leafh of
wenches; he affured Lothario his drawer was
devilifhly honeft, never made a double chalk,
or extravagant bill in all his life; as to Prim
Pimp, the white-headed waiter, (tho' he faid
it that ought not to fay it) in the flefh way,
there was not a better provider in all the
world; your Grace may have here, faid he,

(for

(for he was corned, or mellow) cheaper than
at your Lordfhip's hall, my Lord, of the
fineft relifh, four, or two-footed flefh of
every kind; and, as to my wine—Pray, my
Lord, fhall I get your Grace a bottle, and
fend *Flora* with it, I dare fay your honour
would not like to be waited upon by one of
us the he's—Well, Mr. Fire-face, fays my
Lord, fend your wine and one of your fhe's
—He did fo; my Lord did not relifh the
wine, but he liked the wench, and fo took
her into keeping upon articles; foon he grew
cloyed, took another, then another and another, he fported a variety of new carriages,
had about twenty fervants in fine liveries; he
and his favourite laffes, by turns, rattled
away to mafquerades, plays, balls, routs,
races, and every where; till, by when he was
thirty, his ready cafh was fquandered, his ef-
tates mortgaged, and his body fo emaciated,
enfeebled, and enervated, that had you met,
you might eafily have miftook him for *an old
man of fixty*; it was at this period he bad
Jofeph go and wait for him at the gate.

Now

Now for the fong that Jofeph fung whilft
waiting at the meadow gate.

Lord Lothario make hafte,
Oh that you for once could tafte
The fweet-pleafures of the mill,
Thofe I felt there, and feel ftill;
Here's a heart that's always glowing.
Here are pleafures ever flowing,
Freed from all the noife and ftrife
Of a diffipated life;
Come, Lothario, come away,
Come, or I'll no longer ftay.

On't you, Joe, fays the Peer (who then,
though after the fixed time, arrived at the
gate) well, good manners bid me thank you
for ftaying fo long, ope the gate, may I follow you—Yes, my Lord, fays Jofeph—He
opened the gate, Lothario entered the meadow, and the moment he fet his foot on
that delightful ground he began to contemplate. The Peer and Jofeph walked together (as if equals) the Peer being *incog.*
Jofeph introduced him; they entered the
mill, the family received Jofeph and the
ftranger, and there (reader if you pleafe) we
will leave them, and ftep over to Hodge's
farm to fee what is going forward there.

CHAPTER

CHAPTER V.

Some account of Farmer Hodge *and his family—His wife, fon and two daughters ground—A converfation at Hodge's houfe about grinding —An alarm—A mob at the mill—Fire-face and his crew come to pull it down—The mob drove away by Hodge and his people.*

YOU were told before (reader) that Hodge had employed two or three of thefe young men—They wrought diligently, the farmer was well pleafed, but took no farther notice of them than to fay when they came for their wages, Boys! you are good labourers, there's a fhilling a piece for you above your hire—Dame! tell Audrey to get them a cann of beer; this latter they took if they wanted it, if not they declined it—But as they came into the kitchen at meal times, and con-verfed with the fervants and fome of the family, they were often finging (having good voices) to thofe about them—And afterwards, would talk of the *wonderful Mill, the Chief Operator,* the Rector, Doctor and many

E.   things

things—their converſation—the well known
character of the Rector and Doctor, and many
other things conſpired together ſo, that Hannah Hodge, the Farmer's wife, Robin, his
ſon, Audrey, his eldeſt, and Suſan, his
youngeſt daughter, all had (unknown to
Hodge whilſt he was about his fields) gone
to the meadow and mill; and (in ſhort) pri-
vately paſſed through all the operations* before Hodge was aware of the matter—However, he could but obſerve his Hannah, who,
tho' uſually chearful, would ſometimes be
pittering and pittering about the goings on
at the farm, &c. now ſhe was always eaſy—
Robin too, who uſed to cut and rip, and try
to drive away every thing before him, now
was as meek and mild, as cool and calm as
could be. Audrey, that had a vaſt nack at
dreſſing and ſcolding, reduced her head-
plumes and bridled her tongue; or elſe ſhe
now ſpoke ſo kindly to the maids, that they
all wondered and liked her—Little Sue, a te-
dious peeviſh girl, who before was always
for her own mind, and would cry and bawl
if not pleaſed in every thing, now wore a
conſtant ſmile on her face, and was always

* At this mill perſons of all ages find benefit.

in

in good humour—Hodge wondered what was the matter, but at length he began to fmell a rat (as he call it) had a ftrong fufpicion they had been *a grinding* (as fcoffers by that time began to term it) and he grew angry. Now, though he had a very high refpect for his old friends the Rector and Doctor, yet, conceiving *mean notions of the mill*, and fuppofing that half the time of his family would be taken up there, whilft his farm would be neglected, and all run to rack, he thought within himfelf, after his humorous way,

> Let it be underftood,
> Hodge—nip this in the bud.

For (d'ye mind) fays he to himfelf, if I don't nip off the bud, here will grow a flower by and by (obferve ye) that I fha'nt like the fmell of—So that evening, when the Farmer came home, refolved, right or wrong, to begin upon them—He happened to find his wife and fon Robin looking into an old dufty book by the fire fide, whilft Audrey and Sufan, with the three young men, (the labourers from the mill) were fet near them.

Well, Robin! fays he, have you looked after the horfes? Yes, father! but I fhall fee.

to them again before fupper—Before fupper!
fays Hodge (obferve ye) I doubt you deferve
none, go fee to them now boy—Robin obeyed
—Hark ye, Audrey! have you helped to milk
the cows? Yes, father.—Well, but have
you taken care (mind ye) that the wenches
ftrapped them clean? I am afraid you neglect the bufinefs, and half the cows will
get the gargut, by your lazinefs—Father,
fays Audrey, you never told me I was lazy
before—No, no, you ufed to be well enough,
but I have feen what I don't like, and I fhall
fpeak what you don't like—Here, Sue!—
Papa?—Go hold the lanthorn for Robin 'till
he cleans the horfes—Where's your rock?
what, no fpinning to night?—I have fpun a
fkein, papa—Go, hold the lanthorn, I tell
you, get you gone you little urchin—Sufan
ran ————— a paufe —————
after the paufe, fays Hodge to his Hannah—
Well, wife, (obferve ye) what are you after?
you feem wonderfully mute now a-days—
what book is that you are poring over together, Robinfon Crufoe, or the works of
Fox, the leather-coated quaker? aye, 'tis a
quaker's book I fuppofe, for (obferve ye) for
fome time paft you have been wonderfully
filent;

filent; but, however dame, I'll make you
fpeak—Throw away your book, or I fhall
kick it I know not whither—Here, Prue!
get me a pint of my ftrong ftingo (mind ye)
—bid Robin and Sue come in—Audrey,
where's your cap that coft 7s. 6d. how came
you to have a plain cap and fillet about your
head?—Young men (obferve ye) go home
to your mill, I think to turn ye all off to-
morrow morning—Give me my ftick, wife,
I'll go and fee after my bufinefs myfelf; I
fmell a rat, you are all idle, and the rent of
my farm, and the rates of the parifh, at this
courfe of life, will ruin us all.—Pray, my
dear, fays Mrs. Hodge, what is the matter,
what haft thou been fpending thy market
penny, hufband? what is amifs? all our bufinefs is done, and can there be any harm, after
the toils of the day, to fet down and read the
records of the wonderful mill?—Mill, fays
Hodge, *there's the rub*; aye, that's what I
thought of; why, look ye wife, the mill
will grind all your brains out, if you have
any; but methinks you have been there
before hand; however, wife, though I love
you, and have lived with you thefe thirty
years without a quarrel before, yet now I

tell

tell you, if you attempt to go to the mill a grinding, depend upon it you have done living quietly, or at all, with your old hufband Hodge.

Wife—Wilt turn me out of doors, dear hufband?

Hodge—Doors, no, I love you too well for that yet; but if you want to read, why I have wrote more than you can underftand, or I myfelf either perhaps, Dame (d'ye mind) why prythee read the works of your hufband.

Wife—My dear, your works aim to do good, and your heart I know is honeft, but charity begins at home—firft, get good done to thyfelf hufband; here's a book * gives me more comfort than a thoufand of your writings, and the works of the mill are beyond your comprehenfion.

Hodge—Hark ye, wife, don't provoke me, away with your new noftrums, mind your butter and cheefe, chicks and chickens, and keep your children up to the work—Mark! I love the Rector and the Doctor as well as you do, and have heard (obferve ye) a deal

* The Bible,

of

of talk about the mill, I have been at it,
but never paffed through it, nor do I intend
it, for, d'ye mind, we are not *millers*, and fo
we can't live by grinding.

Wife—My dear hufband, I always was
and always will be yours ; you know I love
you (afk the experience of thirty years) our
children doat upon you, we will all obey you,
except in matters of the mill; but I will
frankly confefs, whatever is the confequence,
my fon Robin, daughter Audrey, myfelf, and
even little Sufan, have all paffed through
the operations, though unknown to you, and
we are happy—the laft and beft of my wifhes
for you, my dear hufband, are, that you
alfo may pafs through, be made as happy
as we are, and then we fhall be all one for
ever.

Hodge—What do I hear? am I in a dream?
what, haft thou been through the mill, and
did you hide it from me?—Well, be it fo,
I have always trufted in my own care, under
Providence, to guide me, I have been honeft as far as I could, have brought up my
family, with the help of God, and you, but
in deep things I know, wife, you are more
ferious, and therefore better acquainted with
fuch

fuch likes than I am; and fo go on, Hannah, go on my children; although I have fpoken in an ill temper, yet I don't fee, to fpeak the truth, that you are altered for the worfe; fo go on I fay. I fhall never go a grinding with you, but, however, we will love one another. Drive on the bufinefs of the farm (d'ye mind) and *every one fhall go his own way*—I'll go inine, fays Hodge. At this inftant the converfation was interrupted by halloo! halloo! Mafter Hodge, Mafter Hodge, and all that are within, come quickly to the mill—there's a great mob around it, and a riot; they are about to pull it down, and threaten to drown the Rector, Doctor, and all the folks there; therefore, you and your people go quickly and repel the mob.

Hodge—The Devil (d'ye mind) feems to be let loofe now a days—give me my crab ftick and conftables ftaff, for I am conftable of the parifh (obferve ye) call Robin—Here, call our men Ralph, Roger, Valentine, Tom —Where's the maids Bridget, Ruth, Margaret, and the reft of you; let the boys be called, Halloo! where are you, Sam, Ned; Tibly, Trimmer, where are the young men of the mill—are they home? here, all of you,

take

take your whips, flails and pitchforks; women take your bruſhes and broom ſtalks;
Audrey and Sue (can you fight with your father?) lay hold of your ſtools, pattens, and
rock ſtaffs; come along—I'll hobble before
you, and lead you to battle—I don't like
your grinding way (mind ye) but I love the
Rector and the Doctor and all about them;
therefore, come along quickly, *we'll never be
governed by a mob*—We'll go and drive them
off the ground, or I'll ſhiver my crab-thorn
and conſtables ſtaff to pieces; and (obſerve
ye) before they ſhall drown my old friends—
(come along) here's old Hodge, who in this
right cauſe will venture his life for them—
Away hies Hodge—all the family and ſervants followed him, the ploughmen and ſervants took their weapons; the wife, children, and young men took none; we leave
them going to reſcue the Rector, Doctor,
&c. and to ſave the mill, &c. mean time we
ought to tell you how the uproar happened.

It happened thus,
Joſeph and the Peer, as you heard before, were
arrived at the mill, where, to the aſtoniſh-
ment of Lord Lothario, he found, by con-
verſing with the Rector, Doctor, the young

F men,

men, and people on the spot, what he had
heard from Joe was true—He became so
charmed with the converſation of theſe people, and profited ſo much by a lecture that
happened to be delivered that evening, that
he reſolved not to go, as propoſed, to the
midnight rout of *Lady Rittle Rattle*, but to
abide with them there at leaſt for that night,
if they would ſuffer him to reſt amongſt
them ; he was ſhewed a room decently
furniſhed, in the *ſilent ward*, which lies
next the ward *oratorial*.—Being ſhewn
to his bed by one of the young men of the
place (who ſoon retired) and being left in
profound *ſilence*, he began to reflect upon the
life of diſſipation he had led from his earlieſt
days, this drove ſleep far from him—his
mind was filled with fear, and that night
he took no reſt; early at the cock-crowing
in the morning, he heard an audible voice in
the ward of oratory; to which, liſtening
with profound attention, he found it was the
Rector in the article of prayer; reſolved
to ariſe, he did ſo, dreſſed himſelf, and went
ſoftly to the ſide of the oratorial ward, near
which ſtood the low ſeat, pedeſtal, or ſtool
(of repentance) he ſet himſelf down upon it,

and

and inftantly found himfelf ftrongly inclined to confefs all that was in his heart—his audible confeffion alarmed the Rector fo, that after morning matins were over, he came to the Peer, examined him as to the prefent ftate of his mind, and having good caufe to hope he was a fincere penitent, allotted him a place in the oratorial ward.

In that ward he continued for fome time, and a report being fpread in the fuburbs that Lord Lothario was got to the mill—Lady Rittle Rattle being difmally difappointed of the Peer's perfonal appearance at her rout—Old Fire-face alfo miffing his gifty gueft, and Prim Pimp, having loft his beft Mafter (as the Miffes of the Bagnio had their golden cull) moreover, it being reported, that if he was indeed gone a grinding, the very art would fall by which they had their ill got wealth.—Fire-face, his Drawer, Pimp, his wenches, a drummer, a brace of butchers and leafh of link boys; (the drummer and boys being hired by the bountiful landlord of the *Jolly Topers*) all confpired to go in batalia to ftorm the mill, bring away the Peer by force, and not only fo, but to pull down the buildings, for fear the faid

mill

mill fhould undermine their trade; and moreover, if they could catch the Rector, Doctor, and the young fellows that had been at
work amongft them, they refolved to drown
them all in their ditch, to prevent farther
mifchief—To this laudable end, having pro-
cured a cart, on which Fire-face placed the
fag end of a butt of beer, to fpirit up his crew
when they came to action; the whole poffe
marched forward—The *Hoft* of the Jolly Topers led the van, Red Nofe, his drawer,
followed, Prim Pimp, and a leafh of profti-
tutes were at their heels; the Drummer next,
with his drum, the Butchers with their marrow bones and cleavers; a hundred idle filly
boys clofed the cavalcade, and they arrived at
the gate of the meadow and fummoned the
men of the mill to furrender at difcretion,
gave them two hours to confider of the matter, fwore, by Bacchus, if in that time they
did not furrender, the mill fhould go down
to the earth, and they would give no quar-
ter, and that the Rector, Doctor, or who-
foever refifted, fhould be inftantly drowned
in the ditch—mean time, boys, fays Fire-face,
to keep up your fpirits and cheer your hearts,
we'll tap and drink this butt of good ale here
                                        —The

—The cup was handed about, they foon got
dreadfully drunk, and then, with all their
force, puſhed open the gate, and entered the
meadow; but, *being drunk, they could not contemplate*; however, they ſtaggered half way
from the gate towards the mill. When
Hodge and all his people (ſome armed as
aforeſaid, others not armed). Hodge at their
head, arrived there, Hodge forgetting his
lameneſs leaped over the hedge, he entered
the meadow and the mill, crying out, halloo!
here! where's my Rector? where's the Doctor? where's all your people? are ye alive?
where's the mob? what's the matter?—The
Rector calmly ſtepped forward, the Doctor
followed, and told Hodge, the mob, with
Fire-face at their head, were then in the meadow drawing near the mill—But, ſays the
Doctor, we have barricaded the door, ſo that
we think they cannot get in—Get in, ſays,
Hodge, (d'ye mind) open the door, Parſon,
that we on t'other fide may get out and have
at them—I don't fancy your mill much, it
makes a deal of outcry, but I love you my
old friends, I think you better than thoſe
that threaten you, and if you be worſe, the
Devil (obſerve ye) muſt be in you—Here,
Robin,

Robin, my fon! where's your pitchfork—
Father, fays he, I don't truft in fuch arms—
You puppy, you! well (fays Hodge) we can
manage it without ye, only open the door
Bob, I long to be at them—Robert did fo;
Hodge and all his armed fervants (who were
but few) marched out, and foon met Mr.
Fire-face with his motley mob, in the meadow—Hodge began to contemplate (fuch
was the nature of the place) but he had not
time to contemplate much, for Fire-face and
his troop were at hand; therefore, Hodge,
having his conftable's ftaff in one, and the
crab ftick in the other hand, called out aloud
—Hark ye every one of you mobbers, monfters, or whatever you are, I command you
in the King's name (d'ye mind) to *halt*, and
before you ftir one ftep farther tell us what
bufinefs you have here, and what ye come
for—Who's that? fays Fire-face, give him
an huzza my boys; halloo! huzza! they
fhouted huzza! huzza! a butt of beer—Fire-
face for ever, and down with the mill; drown
the Rector, duck the Doctor and all the
crew, down with, down with them—When
the noife fomewhat abated, Hodge called
again aloud, Fire-face, where are you?—
Here

Here I am! fays Old Butts, who are you?
what's that Old Hodge? I think I know
your voice—Know my voice, fays Hodge,
yes, and I know you from head to foot, you,
ye fwaggering fwill-tub—how dare you
come here with your fiery face and carbuncle
fnout to deftroy and to kill? if Beelzebub
has an eldeft fon upon earth you are he, you
carry fire in your countenance—Hark ye!
Bridget, give me a match, that I may try
to light it at the end of that fot's nofe, and
burn his empty fcull to afhes—Who have
you got behind you? by the fmell of his
brandy-fcented breath I think 'tis that rafcal
Red-nofe—And who's next? an't it your
Pimp? the gallows, you three villains, have
groaned years for you (obferve ye) you know
I know you, and in the *King's name*, (mind
ye) I command you, one and all of you, inftantly to difperfe, and ftagger to your homes,
or by all the authority of a conftable (who
might charge every body, or any body, to
mufter amongft us) I vow, this ftaff and this
crab ftick, together with the arms my people are furnifhed with, fhall, if poffible, drive
Lucifer out of you; and, moreover, if you
refift, we'll take you prifoners, and fet you

all

all o'the ftocks—I defy you, you old hob-
bling fon for a w——! exclaimed Fire-face,
and with that, threw his pewter tankard at
Hodge's head, which gave him a fevere fous
o'the noddle—Hodge uplifted his ftaff, and
with one ftroke brought Fire-face to the
ground, his foreman encountered Red-nofe,
his fecond man Prim Pimp, his third firft kick-
ed out the bottom of the drum, and fecondly,
drummed upon the back of the drummer
with his fork-fhaft; the female fervants
plucked off hats, caps, pads, cauls, curls,
and every thing from the heads of the lewd
wenches, and fet them a capering with their
rock ftaffs; in fhort, the mob foon drew
back, old Fire-face bawled out aloud, he
was killed already—Red-nofe fcreamed blood!
broken bones! murder! Prim Pimp bent
his marrow bones and begged for his life,
protefted he was let into this fcrape by the
old fcoundrel his mafter, but never would
he, to his laft gafp, procure another wench,
or join another mob if it would oblige the
whole town; for, fays he, my opinion is,
they are all wicked—Lay hold of them!
fays Hodge, lay hold of them! I myfelf
can bafte a dozen of them, put them all in
the

the ftocks!—But by this time feeling the blows, and beginning to grow fober, they all ftaggered out of the meadow; Hodge finding them fled, returned to the mill—The Rector, Doctor, the Peer, young men, and all the family, expreffed their hopes that neither Hodge or his fervants had got harm— Harm! fays Hodge (d'ye fee) we might have got harm enough for all you, for you did us no good; but (obferve ye) I love the Doctor and Rector, and all of you, but your mill makes fuch a noife I advife you to take it down yourfelves, fell the materials, and let us hear no more of the matter.

The Rector and the Doctor fmiled—the young men faid, they wifhed Hodge himfelf was ground—I believe you are all a good fort of folks, faid he, but I don't like grinding; however, whilft I can hobble to defend you they fha'n't knock you o'the head; you do them no harm. So Hodge and his family departed to their farm, and the people at the mill, after entering the oratorial ward, with thankfgiving for deliverance, retired to reft, and from that time their adverfaries were fo abafhed, that they gave up Lothario, and the works of the mill went on in peace.

G   CHAPTER

CHAPTER VI.

A further account of Lord Lothario, and notice of another great perfonage, one Farmer *George, &c. &c. who came to the mill.*

AT the time of the riot, Lord Lothario being in the oratorial ward, heard nothing of the buftle—When at night he was informed of the particulars by the people of the place, he faid—I do not wonder—Fireface and the reft muft be alarmed at miffing me—*Lady Rittle Rattle* too is no doubt difcompofed, as my appearance and purfe, gave life to her midnight revels—but I have done with them all, I feek more of what I never tafted 'till I came here—Peace of mind is the portion I pant for—my conftitution is injured and my cafh fquandered—my real eftate alfo is mortgaged, but I do not defpair —I will pafs through thefe wards, and either return to my poffeffions a new man, or perifh here.

He

He was as good as his word—He paſſed
through all the operations of the mill—he
became a new creature—he reflected much
upon an event that happened in his earlier
days; he had injured a chaſte beautiful young
Lady, of family, though not of fortune, by
breach of his promiſe to wed her—She had
long been pining away as a recluſe on account
of Lothario—Says the Peer I wronged her
then and will marry her now, it is all the
amends I can make her; ſo, with unbounded
thanks to *the Chief Operator*, the Rector,
Doctor, and people of the mill, he departed,
ſending Joſeph before him to tell his people,
their Lord was coming home—ſoon he arrived; he directed Joſeph to ſee, that all
things about him were conducted decently—
His commands were chearfully obeyed, all
things ſmiled around him, peace, regularity,
and ſobriety now met at Lothario's hall—His
old land-ſteward rejoiced—his mortgages
were ſoon diſcharged—he ſent for the amiable
girl, proteſted his penitence, and being again
believed, ſhe gave him her hand, and they
were married—From that period the Bride
and Bridegroom (for ſhe had been at the mill)
went hand in hand, to make themſelves and

G 2   all

all about them (by example and acts of be-
nevolence) honeft, hopeful, and happy; the
iffue of the marriage at prefent is an only
fon—we wifh him to enjoy his father's benefits and his mother's virtues. Old Fire-face,
at the *Jolly Topers*, foon broke (his wife had
not cared much if he had broke his neck,
for he forced her into that lewd way of life)
—Red Nofe, the drawer, drank himfelf to
death—Prim, the pimp, commenced pick-
pocket, and was tranfported—The wenches
at the inn became ftreet-walkers, and were
committed to the houfe of correction, where
we fhall leave them, in hopes of amendment,
to take notice of another great perfon who
came to the mill.

───────────

There lived in a large town hard by the
mill a moft opulent farmer, called by fome
FARMER GEORGE, a truly refpectable perfon, and his dame was one of the moft amiable women in the world; they had a large
family of the lovelieft children the county
could boaft of, and for many years led a life
(as fome faid) of uninterrupted profperity—
but,

but, as the largest lap can never latch a lot
without a crook, fo our farmer and family
anon found, feveral occurrences that grieved
and perplexed them, efpecially the farmer
himfelf, who, it is thought, laid fome of the
difagreeables too near his honeft heart—he became fore vexed, and did not carry the eafe
upon his countenance that heretofore he
wore. Mrs. George (who, by the bye, fome
think, had herfelf been before at the mill,
but fecretly) was the firft who difcovered the
violent agitation of her beloved's mind; fhe
watched his motions with all the tendernefs
of one who thought fhe could not *live* if
he was *loft.*

The farmer, to fhake off the fatigue of
abundant bufinefs, and get rid of a throng of
fervants who perpetually peftered him for
directions, wandered alone thro' part of his
farm-lands, as far as the meadow—the gate
happened to be open, and he walked in—
very foon he began, with greater attention
than ever, to contemplate—A dark cloud,
which at that inftant hung directly over his
head, fo affrighted him, that, to hide himfelf, and get out of the rain, which fell
freely, he ran he knew not where; but ef-
pying

pying one of the *wards* of the mill, to which
he was haſtily approaching, open, he ran
into it for ſhelter; it was the Ward of Trial.
Here the Doctor going his rounds in the
evening, with the Rector, found the diſtreſ-
ſed farmer—both recognized his countenance,
and the Rector inſtantly ſaid—Farmer
George, peace be unto thee—The Doctor,
who attentively obſerved him, approached
with a bow, to feel his pulſe, but George,
inſtead of holding out, lifted up his arm,
and in the anguiſh and flurry of his mind,
knocked down the Doctor flat on his back—
The Rector was a little alarmed at this, but
the Doctor aroſe with a ſmile; I know his
caſe, ſays he—I have received no harm, we
muſt deal gently with him—The people of
the mill hearing a noiſe, ſoon came; they
ſaid they knew and reverenced the farmer—
Mrs. George (his wife) was ſent for, ſhe
flew to her Lord (for ſo ſhe often called him)
George knew *her*—the children, one and all,
ſoon as they heard of the ſtate of their father,
and where he was ſheltered, came running
to the mill; every one eager to ſoften his
ſorrows, and waive his woes; the eldeſt ſon,
a more noble ſpirited youth (ſome juvenile
ſ foibles

foibles apart) the town ne'er faw, was pierced
to the heart with the moſt poignant grief
for his father—The head fervants at the
farm-houſe began to beſtir themſelves, for a
report had reached them, that he was befide
himſelf—A confultation was held—the whole
town was in confternation, moſt men lament-
ed the farmer's hard cafe; many faid, they
were fure he could never recover—in ſhort,
tho' not naturally, yet he was already legally.
dead, and, therefore, another perſon ought
to manage the farm, and who was fo fit as
his *eldeſt ſon*.

Two (or more) of the chief labourers,
however, were of a different opinion, they
faid, whilſt the old farmer was alive, his eldeſt fon had no more right to manage the
bufinefs than the fervants had; they faid, the
leaſe of the farm itfelf would bear them out,
and juſtify them in fo faying—Wilkinfon,
the head man, behaved rudely, and thunderer, the fecond man, roughly, to the fon;
but their behaviour fprung not from an aver-
fion to the heir, but partly from the natural
fear of convulfive changes, which might af-
fect themfelves; and moſtly, from an *attach-
ment to the father*; on thefe accounts, therefore,

fore, they feem very excufable—Some others
of the fervants, however, (out of employment) rigoroufly combated the ftrange doctrine, and infifted upon it, that, according
to the leafe, right reafon, juftice, and common fenfe, during the father's incapacity, the
fon ought to ftand in his fhoes—all was
confufion, for the head men were perfuaded,
if the fon fhould be fuffered to vault into
the father's faddle, if he did not ride over,
yet, he would certainly put *them* out of employment, and take in others—In the in-
terim, the conduct of the heir deferved, and
gained him *univerfal applaufe*; the opennefs
of his heart never appeared before in a point
of view fo applaudably brilliant—*God* fave
my father, fays he, let him live, and whilft
he lives, I am contented to rule, or not rule
—take care of my father!—Mrs. George
would never leave him without compulfion,
and when forced to do fo, her laft look on
her Lord forced out tears; moft of the people at the great town and fuburbs (ftrange as
it may feem) hearing the deplorable ftate of
the head man of the place, mourned, and
drew up many petitions to the *Chief Operator* at the mill for his recovery.

One

(49)

One day it happened, when the ſtewards,
team-drivers, threſhers, and about ſeventy of
the farmer's ſervants were at the mill, con-
ſulting about what was to be done with their
Maſter, Miſtreſs, the *Son* and the farm; Old
Hodge, having heard a deal of ſtrange news,
waddled down to the place, and finding the
Rector, Doctor, &c. bluntly demanded of
them—Where is Farmer George? He is
within, ſaid they, but he is ſadly, you cannot ſee him—But I will ſee him, ſays Hodge,
(d'ye mind) why ſhould I not ?—Becauſe he
has much company with him—Well then
(obſerve ye) ſays Hodge, one more can make
no great difference, I wiſh to ſee him myſelf
(d'ye mind) for I love him—he's not yet got
into your hopper (as you call it) I ſuppoſe,
is he?—No, friend Hodge, ſaid the Rector,
I wiſh he was; but as you are ſo earneſt,
come along, the Doctor and I will introduce
you—They did ſo—Hodge found him ſitting
on a ſofa in the *ward of trial,* and in the ave-
nue all his ſervants were in the act of *argu-
mentation*—Well, ſays Hodge (to the firſt
man he met) how is, where is, my friend,
your maſter?—Honeſt countryman, ſaid the
ſervant, my maſter is *mad*—Ay, ſays Hodge, I

H   do

do not wonder, here's enow of ye (d'ye mind)
to make any man mad—I have been half mad
myfelf fometimes, with fuch folks as you are;
but (obferve ye) I am brought a bit to myfelf
again—where's his wife? where's his fon?
and where's the other children? with their father, faid the fervant—Well then let me peep
at them all (d'ye mind) and fo he did.

Farmer George was fitting in a declining pof-
ture, leaning his aching head on his confort's
bofom; the eldeft fon fet by him in tears, all
the other children were fobbing around him;
the general cry of the whole family was, Oh!
my Lord, my Hufband! Oh! my Father,
my Father!—The fervants, mean time, full
of arguments, were debating, whether *themfelves* or the *fon* fhould carry on the bufinefs
—Look ye! fays Hodge, that there woman
is a charming dame—that youth (d'ye mind,
foibles apart) is a brilliant boy—all them
there lovely children are amiable—and you,
the feventy fervants, may be well enough in
your ways, but I doubt you love *meat* as well
as *mafter*—Look you here! if my friend the
farmer cannot do bufinefs, his fon fhould ftep
into his place 'till he gets well to be fure—
For (d'ye mind) fuppofe I was as he is, if

my

my fervants were to treat my fon as you do his (odds and ends boys) if I got well again, - I fhould never thank you—and depend upon it the youth on't thank you, whether his father lives or dies; but it runs in my headpiece (d'ye mind) that you had better go home, get your fuppers, and take a nap, for (unlefs I augur wrong) if the Farmer be left amongft the folks here at the mill, he will get well again, and drive on bufinefs as brifk, perhaps brifker than ever.

The fervants thought Hodge a ftrange homely fellow, but, however, having done confulting, they retired—The Rector wondered, the Doctor fmiled, Dame George, the heir, and children, returned, for the night, to the farm; the farmer was left with the Rector and Doctor to be quiet in the ward of trial; where, for a time, we fhall leave him, in order that in chapter the 7th we may prefent you with what you don't expect.

CHAPTER

CHAPTER VII.

*A mad scene, &c. &c. or slight view of the
inside of Bethel, alias Bedlam.*

ONE of Farmer George's servants over
officious, firmly believing his master
was mad, concluded bedlam must be the best
place for him, and slyly slipping away from
the mill, steered his course to the great building, solely appropriated for the reception of
lunatics—He rapped at the door, the porter
anon opened it, and he demanded, with a
voice of some authority, a room in the house
for his master; Why, Sir, says the porter to
him, you must speak to the Governor, the
Governor will speak to the Doctor, and the
Doctor will direct the keeper to shew you a
proper ward for your Master, if he thinks
him, when he sees him, an object of charity—Charity! says the servant, we will have
our master well taken care of, but we don't
want charity; we shall pay you well for
Farmer George's lodgings, if you can do
him any good,—but let me be shewn to a
place where he can be taken good care of, for

a better

a better Mafter I fhall never have—Well,
fays the porter, I will call the keeper, you
fhall fee the wards; and if one be empty,
do, but get a ticket from the Doctor, and your
Mafter may be brought here as foon as you
like; I fhall advife you, however, to take a
fhort jacket for him, one that, if it be properly put on, (I'll fhew ye how) will con-
fine his arms and hands, and prevent his
doing mifchief to himfelf or any body elfe;
you pay 10s. 6d. for it, and when it is returned you will have the half-guinea again;
the fervant paid for, and took the jacket on
his arm, the keeper was called, and he took
the fervant with him, and fhew him firft, a
ward, over the door of which, in large Ro-
man characters, was written

The WARD of HOPELESS LOVE.

Let me look in, fays the fervant; the keeper
opened the door; a window without glafs,
high in the wall, difcovered a lovely youth,
all but naked, ftretched on the ftraw; in his
hand he held a curious twifted knot, compofed of the fame materials that conftituted
his bed—The lunatic ftarted upright;—
Well Tom! fays he, where's my Phillis?—.

have

have you brought her ?—we fhall be married
to-morrow;—Look Tom! for my part I am
ready—here's her nofegay, (fhewing the knot
of ftraw) and here's her ring, (holding up
a link of his leg chain)——Come coy Phillis—Where's my father, mother, brother?—
come along to the wedding,—Who are the
Bride's maids, Tom?—tal, de ral.

> Hair fo black, and eyes fo brown,
> Heaving bofom foft as down;
> Lips more red than cherries fine,
> Cheeks whofe blufh will fhame carmine;
> Arms and hands as white as fnow,
> Graces move whene'er fhe go,
> Voice, 'tis mufic's mellow flow.

See! my Phillis; there fhe pafs—Cruel,
coy, but lovely lafs;—Holloo! you there;
Halloo! You have ftolen my wife, kidnap-
pers!-thieves! robbers! I'll fhoot you all to
atoms!—And with that he threw a handful
of ftraw at the head of the keeper, and
George's fervant, and laid down exhaufted.—
Shocked, he paft that, and came to the ward of

DISAPPOINTED LOVE.

There laid a beautiful lafs,—Straw never
before bore fuch tranfient treafure—fhe fcarce

lifted

lifted up her head, but foftly murmured—
Strephon won my yielding heart, and then
he foon forfook me; I fwim here, on a glaffy
fea, and fhall foon fink into an ocean of fire;
—Ah! Strephon, I forgive thee; my loft
love I forgive thee—Nor do I wifh thee to
float upon this fea of glafs—nor to burn in
yon boiling ocean,—Tom! (fays fhe to the
keeper) d'ye know that Strephon has married the old rich widow ?—Well, it was for
her money—but money will not make my
Strephon happy;—I heard the wedding bells
ring, and they have almoft diftracted me—
but—I wifh them well;—good bye Tom.—
She laid down her lovely head;—The keeper
pulled George's fervant away, for he ftood
like a frozen ftatue, and they paffed the other
wards till they came to one called

The WARD of MISTRUST.

In this ward, clofe up of a corner, with his
back towards the door, fat a meagre figure,
fcarcely to be diftinguifhed from a real fkele-
ton; he held between his two hands a fomething the fervant could not tell what, and
therefore he afked the keeper what he held ?
—Why fays the kind keeper, he hugs between

tween his hands his *Idol*, or in other words,
his *Bag of Money*; fpeak to him he'll tell his
own tale:—Well father! fays George's fervant, How go times?—The lunatic firft
clenched his fifts fafter, turned his head, and
leering flyly upon him, muttered, O'Lud!
O Lud! I fhall be ruined, ftarved, perifhed!
—I have loft already *a fhilling* out of my bag,
—Give me the fhilling, pray give me my fhilling!—I cannot fpare it—rags and ruination—
I fhall not have enough to carry me to the end
of my journey, I fhall come to the workhoufe, and if I do I am refolved directly to hang
myfelf!—Never you miferable mifer, fays
George's fervant, unlefs fomebody gives you
a halter.—And then old hunks was left, with
lefs regret, and they foon came to

The WARD of AMBITION.

In this ward, a ftrong robuft perfon, rather
in years, (a player by profeffion) was found:
he wore a moft monftrous high cocked hat,
decked with feathers, and his coat was gar-
nifhed with pieces of gilt Dutch paper—He
was walking to and fro, in a moft commanding manner, and as foon as he faw the keeper
and

and George's fervant, he exclaimed, Hear!
flaves! hear! know your mafter! know ye
rafcals that I am Lord of Lapland—I married
the Auguft Princefs—Ruttee—Rodunta—
Roundelay—Rumpus—Imperiality; fhe bore
me feven children, all of them, except one,
are dead, but in the calendar they are—tranflated to the fkies, and fhine there as planets
of the firft magnitude; my chief Lord, the
Lord Lowftrings, aiming at my throne, confpired againft me to un-king me, and put me
to death, but I defeated him, and flew, with
my own arm, ten thoufand rebels upon the
fpot. The *Country Boors,* however, thought
I oppreffed them, and, therefore, they alfo
rofe up in arms againft me, they overpowered,
and then banifhed me from my Queen, my
child, my empire, and my all; fo here I am
in a ftrange place, Tom, where all I can do
is, to fing out my miferies —————————
after a long paufe (the Player, or) the Man
of Ambition fung the following

SONG,

Ranta-Tanta, Roar'em Ranta,
Flafhes, flames, and forrows plenty,
Waters, winds, and fnow ftorms dafh us,
Rocks and hills and mountains crafh us;

I   Now

Now we're tofs'd on burning feas,
Now knock'd down by falling trees;
Lapland Witches—fhrivell'd Wizzards,
Burn our hearts and freeze our gizzards.

But, Tom! I will be King over Lapland
after all, or I'll lofe my whole fortune—
Keeper! get me my crown, fceptre, and ring,
—I fhall hold a Court to day.   He faid fo—
threw up his hat, and marched again moft
majeftically—The fervant of George, afto-
nifhed at what he had feen and heard, returned the jacket, took the half guinea again,
and faid to himfelf—My Mafter fhall never
come here; I'll return to the mill, and fee
what is become of him.

CHAPTER

CHAPTER VIII.

Some further account of Farmer George—*of his wonderful recovery—And of other matters.*

BE pleafed to recollect, retentive reader, that at the end of Chapter the 6th, we left the good Farmer George in the ward of Trial, with the Rector, the Doctor and the people of the mill—we now return to him, and are charged by the attendants there to inform you, that for the firft few weeks he bore his trials varioufly; at fome feafons he was penfive and patient, at others obftreperous, or outrageous; fundry practitioners voluntarily offered their fervices—others were called in and fent there by the head labourers at the farm—the family were all anxiety for the event—divers confultations were held—fundry different experiments tried —fome infinuated, that it was improper to call him *Farmer George*, or to approach or treat him as a *fuperior*; others infifted, that

I 2   he

he ought to be treated, and muſt and ſhould
be treated with tenderneſs and profound reſpect, and that at all events his ſervants ought
to be kept at a diſtance, (one or two favou-
rites now and then excepted) and that they
ought not to be ſuffered to teaze him about
their ſeveral oppoſite modes of carrying on
the buſineſs ; at length the latter, for a time,
prevailed—He was humoured often, and he
began (at the time a report prevailed he was
dead, or all but dead) again to become calm,
and to lift up his revered head—the Rector
moved to place him in the *oratorial* ward,
the Doctor acquieſced, and intended from
thence to conduct him to the *watch* and
other *wards*—the young men and people at
the mill argued ſtrongly to have him paſs
through *all* the works—He was led forth to
the river, and drank; to the rivulet, and
taſted of the ſtreams; he became almoſt in-
ſtantaneouſly invigorated—He propoſed to ſit
down on the ſeat or pedeſtal, to paſs thro'
the mill, and then, ſays he, *farewell farm*, I'll
yield the buſineſs to my eldeſt ſon—My
land, fertile in itſelf, by unſkilful manage-
ment in ſome of my former ſervants, have
brought forth two many briars and thorns—
may

may my fon's hufbandry bring forth better things. We have a good cottage on the borders, that will do for my dear dame, my youngeft children, and myfelf—I will retire, and live upon a fmall portion of the profits of my farm in peace—Dame George, hearing her hufband's wifh, came into the fcheme—the youngeft children confented— the plan was ripening for execution, when lo! the chief labourers, who had gained intelligence of the plan, came in a body to the mill—they rejoiced (they faid) that their mafter was better—they were fure it would be improper and impolitic in him to decline bufinefs; they averred, that he was now well able to hold the reins again—and even if his nerves (at times) fhould be found feeble; their ftrong hands fhould help him—In fhort they infifted upon his immediate removal from the mill—the Rector advifed—the Doctor remonftrated—the people on the fpot implored, that the farmer might not be taken away till he had received the *full benefit* of the mill-operations; but it was all to no purpofe; the fervants had *(a priori)* brought with them the farm carriage to the fpot, they had previoufly prevailed upon their dame and

young

young mafter to accompany them, and join
in folicitations for his removal to the farm;
the farmer overcome by intreaties, having
the good of *all* at heart, yielded to be taken
from reft and retirement again, to walk in
thofe weighty ways of bufinefs, which before had been too heavy for his feeble frame
—However, juft before his departure, at the
very inftant he was about to mount his
farm curry, Farmer Hodge, on foot, came
up to the mill, and finding his fervants in
the act of removing the *great farmer;* exclaimed—Hark ye! what is my friend
George agoing? Let me afk a queftion (obferve ye) *has he been ground down here?*—Is
he young and ftrong again? why, Mafter
(Hodge) anfwered Wilkinfon, Thunderer,
and the reft of them, he's got fo ftrong, that
he can do his bufinefs well enough, with
our help; and he is not fo *old* yet as to re-
quire grinding—Well! well! replied Hodge,
but truly I have heard and feen fo much of
this here mill, that I intend to be ground
myfelf, and I wifh your mafter to be ground
rightly before he goes, but if that can't be,
then I pray ye, that half a fcore of you his
trufty fervants, who, by the look of ye (d'ye
mind

mind) appear old enough for grinding, would abide here a bit, by way of good company, and ftep (obferve ye) into the hopper with me myfelf, fo that we may (mind ye) all be ground together, we can hardly grind for the worfe boys—But all the fervants (a very few excepted) anfwered, our full employment at the farm takes up our heads and hearts too much to beftow a thought about his grinding mill, and, moreover, Mafter Hodge, we are not yet old enough for grinding—An't you? fays Hodge, you may have a mill upon your yonder great farm; and belike fome fay, you have, and that moft of you are too *old* for us all, becaufe you take too much toll of your cuftomers; but then (d'ye mind) however that may be, take my advice, and henceforth don't grind your poor neighbours fo hard, left by overgrinding you fet your mill faft and hurt your trade fo much, that they in their turn may make themfelves millers, and grind you. One of the moft talkative of George's tribe ftepped forward to Hodge, and faid, old hobbler, look at my countenance—poor old fellow, your eyes are dim, or you might fee in a moment that I am perfectly young yet—

Boy,

Boy, (returned Hodge) dim as my eyes are, I can fee that foft pulpy place in your fcul-cap, and dare venture to vouch for you, (Mr. Impertinence) that you are like to be young as long as you live, child.

Here the converfation ended—Farmer George, the family and fervants, drove away, and, tho' ftrange to fome, yet certain it is, he received fo much benefit at the mill, that from the day of his return to this day he has been enabled to conduct and carry on his bu-finefs, as well, perhaps better than before.

N. B. Pity he was not fuffered to go thro' (as he wifhed to do) all the operations of this wonderful mill.—

The grateful Farmer George rewarded the Doctor and people at the mill *moft boun-tifully.*

CHAPTER

CHAPTER IX.

Lord and Lady Fashion—A Philosopher and a brace of Lawyers come to the mill—Curious conversation pieces, &c.

WELL-founded reports of the recovery of the great Farmer, Lothario, and sundry others, so filled the minds of the men on the other side the mill, that prodigious numbers came up to the meadow gate to reconnoitre its scite and situation, and so many opened and shut, and shut and opened it, that by order of the *Great Operator*, signified to the Rector, Doctor, and the rest at the mill, a porter was stationed there with orders to examine all those who asked admission, previously to their entering the meadow—One of the aforesaid young men was appointed to the important office, whose name was *Peter*; he took his station with a willing mind, and had the charge of the keys, for the gate had a double lock—Soon after he was fixed there, numbers of *thinking* people came, all of

K   whom

whom were readily admitted, moſt of them were ground down, and returned with joy; others came only to gaze and to hear— Amongſt whom were the following cha- racters :

A Lord and a Lady of Faſhion.

A Lord and Lady of faſhion came lolling in their chariot and ſix to the gate—a laced footman, finer than even his maſter, came galloping up before them, and ordered the ſaid Peter to open the gate directly, for, ſays he, the carriage will be here in a moment— Pray, ſays Peter, whoſe carriage is it?— You blunt fellow you, ſays he, open the gate, 'tis the illuſtrious Lord and Lady Fa- ſhion's chariot—I'll wait till it comes up, ſays Peter—ſo he did—it was ſoon there— and his Lordſhip, more civil than his ſervant, requeſted the porter to open the gate, that he and his Lady might take a turn in the mea- dow, and view the mill; for, ſays his Lord- ſhip, we have heard much of the mill, and if the thing be faſhionable it ſhall have our patronage.

Great Sir, ſays Peter, the faſhion of the mill is truly *good,* but 'tis very *old,* and we ſeldom find people of faſhion paſs through
it

it—However, he opened the gate, and the carriage entered the meadow—his Lordſhip and the Lady were drove up to the mill—but the Peer, having an engagement at the Taylor's to fit a laced levee ſuit, and her Ladyſhip at the milliner's, to pop on a French-faſhioned cap, they declared upon their honours it was impoſſible at that time either to alight or ſtop, and therefore, the vehicle being turned round, they were drove out of the meadow; but, however, before they reached the gate, contemplation ſo far overtook them, that his Lordſhip ſaid, he thought the mill a good contrivance for ſome ſort of people, and my Lady added, it may be ſo for the meaner claſſes, but the ſituation (ſays ſhe) is ſo low my Lord, and the meadow ſo moiſt, that I have caught my death here already, or, if I live, I ſhall not be able to ſee company this fortnight—Let the fellow drive home my Lord—I ſhake already, and am afraid, by the effects of this meadow (of contemplation) I ſhall ſoon be ill; pray, my Lord, let us get out of this bog, and if I ſhould live to get home, I am reſolved never to come again a grinding—Why it is a ſtrange place, anſwered my Lord, I feel I know not

K 2   how

how myfelf—Drive on! John—So they returned—and the men of the mill faw them
no more.

The next who entered was a hair-brained
Philofopher—he came with a moft profound
and fagacious air—What is your name, Sir?
(fays he to the Porter)—Peter!—Oh, Peter,
I have read in an old volume of a name-fake
of yours, who wore a girdle about his loins,
on which was fufpended a brace of keys;
but I believe no fuch fables; pray how old
are you? Old enough to be better than I am,
fays Peter, but not old enough to think myfelf fo worthy as the Peter you talk of—Ig-
norant fellow, fays the Philofopher, I have
made nature my ftudy for at leaft thefe fifty
years, philofophy, chemiftry, and a hundred
other curious arts are as eafy to me as telling
my fingers —you have got here a new noftrum
of a mill, to delude the vulgar and impofe
upon the credulous, by making them believe, if they are ever fo old, they may be
ground young again—I am come not to *try*,
but to *fee* and examine the parts, and confute
the

the whole procefs of your mill; and before
I enter the meadow, if you'll tell me your
age I'll difclofe to you fomething more rare
and fingular than all the fecrets of your fa-
mous machine.—Sir, fays Peter, (with all
your learning, I queftion if you *know yourfelf*, however) I fhall be 57 years of age next
July—Well then (fays the man of philofophical experiments) you have paffed through
at leaft five revolutions—all your exterior
parts are renewed without grinding, about
once in ten years, or lefs, by nature—your
head, hair, heart, loins, legs, feet, your every
thing, are not the fame they ufed to be—the
old ones are evaporated, and new ones fprung
up in their places—your head, you fee, is
half as big again as it was forty-feven years
ago—you have loft your locks—they firft
were flaxen, next brown, and thofe now on
your fcalp are half of them whiteifh; anon
your head (when thefe fly off) will be covered
with hollow tubes, as white as fnow; your
heart is vaftly altered from what it was—
worn down thefe laft thirty years, by ac-
tions fyftole and diaftole, taking in and pump-
ing out the blood—affifting the ftomach in
boiling down the food and ftewing what you

eat

eat till it becomes chyle, &c. forcing the
red fluid of life, in which the foul (fo called)
lodges, through all the veins, &c. I fay, by
this continual labour it has fent away itfelf,
and another, and another, in rotation, has
fucceffively taken up its place, fo that your
prefent heart is not yet ten years old—Your
loins have been replaced with new ones five
times over, and as to your hands and feet,
why, they are no more the fame hands and
feet they ufed to be than your nails are the
fame nails—and you know yourfelf (don't
ye) if you chip your (corns and) nails once a
fortnight, they will be chipped away in the
courfe of one year, one month, three weeks,
fix days, twenty-three hours, fifty-nine mi-
nutes, and forty-nine feconds, according to
the accurate account or calculation of Monf.
de Ranta Tanta, nail-cutter to the Grand
Monarch ; therefore, thofe under your gloves
and ftockings muft be new ones, not a for-
tieth part fo old as yourfelf—And fo I argue,
that you are not the fame Peter you formerly
was, five Peters at leaft have had your appearance—and in ten years more you will be fuch
another kind of Peter, that he who fees you
now will not know you (if he fees you then,
nor

nor will you be known exactly till you get round again.

And pray, Sir, fays Peter, have I any immortal part about me?

Immortal! alas poor filly man (anfwered the Philofopher) if by immortal you mean the *foul*, I told you before it was lodged in the blood, and if the blood runs all out of the body, as Ariftotle wifely obferved, the foul will be left behind to *pick ftraws*; why, in one fenfe of the word, all things (as he affirms) even the world itfelf is immortal, that is, it will endure for ever—For by a lucky affemblage of combining atoms, drove by a chance wind in hotch potch together, this world was made, and fo long as faid winds blow (and they will blow for ever) the world will be fuftained. As to the romantic ftories you have heard of its being drowned by water heretofore, and of its being to be burnt by fire hereafter, they are arrant forgeries, delufions and cunning prieft's cheats; for the truth is, *all things are material* (as Doctor Prieftley avows)—Why, Peter, the world itfelf is made up of materials, fome of them much like ore, or clay. The bodies of men, beafts, infects, and even vegetables are alfo made

made up of materials; and even your foul itfelf is as furely made up of matter, as the
foles of your fhoes are compofed of a bark-
impregnated ox-hide—You are and muft
be immortal as well as I, and all others are;
for we can prove by chemical demonftrable
operations, and by (pounding) decompound-
ing, or analyfing bodies, that they are all
made up, or conftituted, of certain com-
bined matters, that is to fay, of earth, water,
fire, oils, and certain falts, all which came
from fomewhere, and when, by unforefeen
accidents or changes, they fhall be feparated again, they go fomewhere—Nothing
will be annihilated, for depend upon it, part
of your body will return to earth, part to
air, part to fire, part (perhaps the largeft
part) to water, part to oil, and part to falts
or fulphur. As to your foul, as you call it,
it is nothing at all but fiery, or phlogifti-
cated air, which came from the original fire,
and will return, when quenched (that is
when you die, Peter) to the faid original
fountain of fire, and there remain, 'till by a
lucky blow of fate's, or nature's bellows, your
conftituted parts will be re-united, and a
thoufand years hence you may ftand again at
this

this gate, if it abides fo long, exactly the fame man you are now, Peter.

Well, fays Peter, many are the errors of this age, but from your philofophical frenzies,

Good Lord Deliver us.

Go to the mill, you will find plain honeft youths there, who will prove, to your fhame, your notions are chimerical, and yourfelf the dupe of them.

A Lawyer, commonly called Mr. Sampfon Smart, alias Quirks, the attorney, next came to the gate and demanded of Peter an opening; the porter, by his green bag and parchment fcrolls, guelfed his profeffion, and gently requefted for what end he wifhed to enter—You, Sir, fays he, none of your interrogatories, I am a Gentleman of his Majefty's Court of —————— and am continually fuppofed to be in Court, only in matters of infinite neceffity I get leave of abfence for eleven months in the year, or, more, to fcrape up, create, or get employment, and being often overwhelmed with bufinefs fo much, that if I could be cut and fplit as often as a polype, every part would have double employment; I now hafte

L   here

here, almoſt out of breath, for I have twenty
more engagements to day—I ſay, I haſted.
here to give notice, that the people of yonder
place have inſtructed me to diſpoſſeſs the
crew who harbour on this notorious ſpot,.
and therefore I command you to, ope the
gate, that I may walk in the meadow, view
the mill, and take my meaſures to bring an
ejectment, in which, like all other fictions
in law, I ſhall declare all I pleaſe, and prove
all I can againſt your Rector, (Quack) Doctor, and all your fraternity; and in the end
turn you out of poſſeſſion, ſo that I may procure peace to the country, and veſt the pre-
miſes in the original right owners and their
heirs—And mind this, you Mr. Porter, as
this mill was erected in that meadow by you
and others the conſpirators, before you iſſued.
or ſued out the ancient writ of *ad quod dam-
num*, I am as ſure to carry the cauſe at the
bar, as my clients are to keep their coats on
their backs.

The moment Peter heſitated about opening the gate to Mr. Quirks, came from the
mill up to ſaid gate another lawyer, who
had been ground there many years before,
and who very frequently reſorted to the mill,

and

and converfed with the people; his name
(given him by his employers) was, Bartho-
lomew Black-fwan, he lived on accommo-
dation fquares, and was up to the chicanery
of Quirks—Peter who knew him, with a
low bow repeated the aforefaid converfation,
and afked whether he fhould ope the gate to
Quirks, or deny him entrance—My friend,
Peter, fays Black-fwan, ope the gate, let him
enter, it may do him good—but before he
comes into the meadow, I'll fpeak to him—
He did fo, and the following converfation enfued between the two lawyers.

Quirk—Oh! the gate is opened, I fee, to
let you out, but, Mr. What d'ye call your
name, Why not *let me in*, Sir?

Black-fwan—You have fo often let in
others, Mr. Quirks, that I wonder you
fhould afk to be let in yourfelf.—*Quirks*,
Pray, Sir, who are you?—Why, Sir, I'll
come to you on that fide the gate, perhaps
you will then remember that you have feen
me before; Black-fwan did fo—Oh, Sir,
cried Quirks, I am glad to fee you, two of
a trade don't always agree, but you and I
will never differ again, and, therefore, I'll

be

be fo open as to tell you—I have orders from
my clients to bring ejectments againft the
people at the mill, and I was juft now telling the Porter fo—I am infinitely happy to
meet you Mr. Black-fwan on the very fpot
—and if you will affift me with your advice, here will be pretty pickings for us
both, and if we get the caufe *(inter nos)*—
we will go fnacks—you fhall have one half
of the profits, I the other; and, moreover,
Sir, I fhall hold myfelf obliged to you as
long as I fhall be able to fupport and practice *the glorious uncertainty of the law*—Mr.
Quirks, replied Black-fwan, I have been a
lawyer, profeffionally, more than thirty years
—I have fometimes undertook, as moft lawyers do, matters I did not fully underftand,
nor is it perhaps poffible for the moft pene-
netrating mind, affifted by the moft retentive
memory, to receive, digeft, and infallibly de-
termine upon all the innumerable, nice, and
difficult points of law—Judges, themfelves,
frequently differ in opinion—and an omni-
fcient lawyer, who underftands the whole
(though one lately dead was flatteringly fo
ftyled) is not to be met with under Heaven
—But

—But we all know how to be *honeft*, and to make doing by others as we wifh to be done by, our *pole ftar*—A lawyer, of this caft, will always be fupported; I have found it fo in a greater degree than I ever merited; my lei- fure hours, which were not too many, ad- mitted me to ftudy the memoirs of the mill —I have gone through all the operations— I am now happy, and more convinced than ever, a quirking lawyer is an harpy, who fucks the very vitals of plaintiff, defendant, or both, the peft of fociety, or, in other words, a legal pick-pocket—I know you well—you are of that fable complexion, and therefore, I advife you, Sir, to drop this unjuft and vexatious law fuit, or if you dare to proceed, I fhall efpoufe the honeft caufe of all the peaceable people at the mill— my duty, Sir, will compel me to defend them.

Quirks—My dear Mr. Black-fwan, you feem to be in earneft, but you totally mifun- derftood me—I did not mean to proceed un- lefs you would have affifted me (and why will you not?)—I fay again, we might fo *ma- nage matters*, as to put fome money into

both

both our pockets, *whoever gets the cause,* but I fee you are on the other fide of the queftion—fo I'll go to my clients—give them my bill, and (if I can) get the money —I will never oppofe you Mr. Black-fwan, I admire your character, and would follow it, but my mafter, with whom I was clerk, has a thoufand times told me, *an honeft law-yer cannot live*—Be that as it may, I drop the caufe againft the folks at the mill, and I am Mr. Black-fwan, Sir, your moft obe-dient, humble fervant.

The Lawyers parted,

And we now part with this the 9th to begin the 10th Chapter.

CHAPTER

CHAPTER X.

An account of a remarkable quaker who came
to the mill—an interefting conteft between
him and Hodge—other perfons approach-
ing, &c.

AFTER the departure of the lawyers, a
decent dreffed perfon approached the
gate—there was a certain fomething fo fingular in his appearance that it feems worth
while to defcribe his perfon—his drefs—his
converfation—and his behaviour. ᛁ

As to his perfon, it was rather tall—his
locks were grey, his forehead high and open,
his eyes brilliant, nofe aquiline, complexion
fair, lips vivid, chin fmooth, head fmall,
and his face long; but his countenance was
remarkably ferious—commanding and re-
fpectful; from the fhoulders downward he
was well proportioned, fymmetry feeming to
fet fmiling on his perfon, his fteps were
grave, and all his movements graceful—His

drefs

dreſs vied with that of a Prince in cleanli-
neſs and neatneſs, though not in embroidery
or price—a large jetty broad-brimmed beaver
covered his ſteady head, his neckcloth and
linen where white as ſnow; his coat, waiſt-
coat, and breeches were light drab, with a
tinge, or hue of the olive; his ſtockings
paired his garb; his ſhoes were plain black,
and neatly tied with thong-leather; his
gloves white, and his ivory-headed cane ſup-
ported his right hand, in which he held his
glove, whilſt the left hand was concealed
by its fellow, both gloves were formed of
thin kid-ſkin—in ſhort, he was what the
folks without call *a Quaker*; when he came
up to the gate, his converſation with Peter
was as under:

Quaker—Peace be to thee friend—ope thy
portal if thou pleaſeſt, that I may enter and
ſee the ſons of peace at the mill.

Peter—I muſt examine thoſe who wiſh to
enter, therefore, though your appearance is
truly venerable, yet I pray you to tell me
who you are?

Quaker—I am a friend.

Peter—A friend, to whom?

Quaker

Quaker—To all the people upon earth, but efpecially to thofe who have gone through the inward works, and who faithfully abide at the mill.

Peter—Have you been at this mill before?

Quaker—I have, friend, and hope ever to be thankful—the mill ground me years ago; it is truth, I fell on a ftone there and was broken, had that ftone fallen upon me it would have ground me to powder—But I was made whole—I have ever fince been led in the right way, and I remain (through favour) whole to this day; ope the portal, I pray thee, friend, that I may enter and fee the Rector, the Doctor and all the friends at the mill—I wifh to commune with them again before I depart from this tabernacle, and to leave at the place a token of gratitude to the Chief Operator there, that the dwellers on the fpot hereafter may know, the works of the mill are not the works of vanity or folly.

Peter foon opened the gate—the Quaker walked up, and found a warm reception—the Rector, Doctor, young men, and all the people there (Hodge excepted) foon knew him, and they welcomed him. But it fo

M   happened

happened that Hodge ftumping in foon after, the current of converfation was quickly
turned, for Mafter Hodge rather abruptly began upon the Doctor thus—

Hodge—Look ye here, Mafter Doctor, I
came to fee you and the Rector to-day, and
(obferve ye) I have had fome inkling of being ground myfelf, but (d'ye fee) I always
choofe my company—I can pafs through
with thofe fort of people I like well and
good, but if not, I fhall e'en give up the matter (obferve ye) for it runs in my noddle, that
(as I told my wife Hannah) *under the rofe*,
you are all *Quakers*—I wifh for the Gentleman's excufe, but pray mafter ftranger let
me afk you if you are not of a leathern family—I mean (d'ye mind) are you not a-kin
to *George Fox*, who was a rank (and belike
the firft) Quaker ?

Quaker—Friend I know thee not—and
thy blunt language might give fome offence
did I not know how to put up with it—
but I was taught at the mill that patience
which hath been of much ufe to me, and
may'ft be of fome to thee, for I fhall an-
fwer with that meeknefs thou canft not
claim nor well expect; and if thou wilt hear,

I feel

I feel *an opening* to tell thee the things
which belong to thy prefent and future
peace.

Hodge—Hark'e, Mafter Stranger, we ufed
to be quiet enough, and every one jog on his
own way, 'till this here mill came in vogue,
but fince that (d'ye mind) our peace has been
broken in upon by hurly burlies, mobs and
outcries; you talk about peace, but, obferve,
I am conftable of the parifh, and have had
much to do of late to reftore the King's
peace—But don't flide from the point, an-
fwer the queftion, are you not a relation of
old Fox the Quaker?

Quaker—Not after the flefh, or family, as
'tis called, but I have been led by the fame
light, and have received the fame *fpirit*, and
the fame confolation, Friend George Fox
did.

Hodge—Confolation, ay, ay, I have heard
(obferve ye) a great deal of prattle about
confolation, and I have been hunting after it
thefe thirty years—D'ye mind, ftranger, I
have wrought hard in my time, paid every
man to a penny, brought up my family (a
pretty large one) have never bilked my labourers who cut my corn and did my farm

M 2   work—

work—I have helped the poor as well as I
could, and have paid the Parſon's tithe too
—but, after all, I never could catch that
ſame conſolation. And ſince this here mill
has been ſet a grinding, we have had ſo
much pother, and my mind (d'ye ſee) have
been ſo puzzled and peſtered, that I am farther off than ever; in ſhort, my wife, boys
and girls, who ſay they have been ground
here, have a great deal unhinged and unſet-
tled me—to be ſure I have food, drink, and
rayment ; I can pay my rent too, but I want
ſomething, I know not what (obſerve ye)
to give me conſolation—Methinks, if this
ſame mill was removed, and my ears no longer
filled with grinding operations by my ſaid
wife, the Rector, Doctor, and fifty more
of thoſe ſort of folks, I ſhould come to my
old centre again, and be ſatisfied.

Quaker—Friend, I believe thou haſt ſought
conſolation from thine honeſty, uſefulneſs, and
the things of this world—Honeſty and uſefulneſs are good, ſo far as they go, but they do
not go far enough, nor can they together
yield thee *inward* conſolation ; turn the eye
of thy mind, friend, to the *light within thee*,
then ſhalt thou ſee clear, and be led in the
way

way of *truth*. Moreover, thy heart fhall be
tendered by refrefhings from on high—thou
fhall foon come out of Egyptian darknefs,
and walk in the true light of life—I will
converfe with thee, if thou pleafeft, more
at large on thefe good things, but obferving
thou makeft it a part of thy boaft that thou
payeft *tithes* to thy Parfon, I muft bear my
teftimony againft that hireling practice, and
declare unto thee, friend, thou fuffereft by
paying; yea, that it is unlawful to pay the
tenth of thy increafe, commonly called
tithes.

Hodge—Hey day! what! I thought you
had been a friend to our Rector at the mill
(d'ye mind).

Quaker—So in verity and uprightnefs I
am, I efteem the Rector and all at the mill fo
far as they efteem the truth, and when any
errs, he is the beft friend who bears his teftimony againft errors—Thy Rector, in fome
points, may err. His certain ceremonies at
yonder fteeple-houfe, and his taking *tithes,*
feem to me to be errors, and, therefore, I
bear my teftimony (I tell thee) againft fuch
practices.

Hodge—

Hodge—Look ye here, as to the steeple-
house, as you call it (observe ye) my father,
grandfather, and all my family ('till some
of them of late went a grinding) were
staunch churchmen, so am I myself a
churchman to the bone, though, to tell you
the truth I seldom go there; but, however, on Sundays I read my book at home,
smoke my pipe, drink a pot of stingo with
Tom Trylands, the farmer, and consult
what is best to be done the other six days of
the week—I don't frequent tap-houses (observe ye)—I don't swear, nor, in the lewd
way, did I ever go astray—All my children
have been *christened,* and some of the first
folks of the town (mind ye) were *godfathers*
and *godmothers* to my boys and girls;
few better christians could been found in the
country than they were, 'till it came into
their nappers to go to the mill a grinding—
since when they chatter about happiness and
I know not what, at so strange a rate, that I
cannot augur what has betided them.

Quaker—Friend, thou sayest thou art a
staunch churchman; I testify unto thee, the
true church is not composed of bricks,
mortar,

mortar, wood and lead, but of very different materials.

Hodge—True, (obferve ye) you are right,
our church is built with great ftones, daubed
over with clay, and covered with ftraw;
as to the feels, the fpars, and fome of the
feats, they are wooden enough (d'ye mind)
and rotten enough too; for if you could eat
after moths, maggots, and worms, you
might crumble fome of the wood-work
into your difh of pottage.

Quaker—And, therefore, thou canft believe, that the church or fteeple-houfe, can
enter the kingdom of Heaven?

Hodge—No, it will foon (d'ye mind) tum-
ble down to the earth, unlefs our towns-
folks could be forced to repair it, but, however (obferve ye) 'tis up-hill work to get money out of pockets where none is got in;
and our people fay (efpecially my brother
fmall farmers) they have enough to do to pay
high rents, *heavy taxes*, and *large rates*, to
maintain the poor; without building new,
or repairing old churches; and, for my own
part, I fhould not be troubled much, if the
church was blown down, fo that the fteeple
was left ftanding, and our fine peal of eight
bells

bells left behind; I fhould not like to lofe the *bells*, for I have often tugged a rope at a peal of *bob-majors*, and am vaftly proud of ringing.

Quaker—Thy mind is carnal—thou canft not, or wilt not, underftand me—I will therefore tell thee plainly, thou haft more humour than ferioufnefs, and thou pretend-eft thou doft not, becaufe thou wilt not un-derftand me.

Hodge—Hark ye, Mafter Quaker, don't turn out queer, I did underftand you in part, and I owned our parifh church (obferve ye) fooner than climb up to Heaven, would fall down to earth.

Quaker—But I teftify unto thee, the ftee-ple-houfe, built with bricks, mortar, wood, ftraw, and fo forth, is not a church.

Hodge—What a'nt it a church? But I fay (obferve ye) it is a church, our true parifh church; and fo long as it ftands it will and fhall be a church—you will not fwear I dare think, that it is a Quaker's meeting-houfe?

Quaker—Friend, I obey the command— "Swear not at all"—But I wifh thee to be ferious—come to *inward ftillnefs*, and thou may'ft may'ſt be convinced, that the true church, is conſtituted of *living ſouls*, ſpiritualized through divine favour, and made meet (or making meet) to become living ſtones of that ſpiritual building (far grander than Solomon's Temple) of that building, that is called, " *God's Houſe*," ſuch ſtones are the true people at this mill.

Hodge—Obſerve ye, I am not a *free maſon*, poor Hodge, knows no great matters about building, he knows ſomething, however, about repairing, and he hopes that his Landlord will ſoon thatch his old barn, ſo that his corn may be kept dry; and as you were talking about *not paying tithes*, and ſaying it was unlawful to pay them, if you can put me in a way to with-hold them (d'ye mind) *honeſtly*, I'll run up a lean-to againſt my barn's gable, at my own coſts, to lay my next year's crop of tithes in.

Quaker—Our friends in general look upon the payment of tithe as a matter of *ſuffering*, and therefore with-hold them from the hireling prieſts, though ſometimes they are ſeverely proſecuted and forced to yield to, or loſe by *Proctors* and *Lawyers* (the Miniſters of the *Spiritual Court* ſo called) more than

N   the

the Priefts themfelves, in the firft inftance, would have demanded of them.

Hodge—Hark ye, Mafter Quaker, Hodge loves to be open, and will be open to you— When we had a Rector, an old, learned, lazy, mufty bachelor, cloiftered up in a College, who took no more care of our fouls than *Pope Joan* does, but who took care, however, to peep at us once a year for the tithes, worth about 200l. and charitably allowed his poor bare-boned Curate, out of his gain, 25l. per annum, and furplice fees, for the cure of all our fouls—I was wont to laugh at the Doctor and to pity his Curate—True it is (d'ye mind) my tithe at that time, let out and taken by a *grey-coated Parfon*, to the laft furrow, or fheaf, went from me unwillingly; but the Curate's fees I always paid cheerfully for marrying and burying all the poor when I was overfeer; and for the moft part I myfelf took the gownfman home to partake of a family dinner—My fon Robin is about to be married, and though, when his wife has children, it will coft *threepence per child* to chriften them, that is to make them, as we fay, children of God, and heirs of the kingdom of Heaven, yet, as matters are
like

like to go with us poor farmers, I hope my son will ſtrive to pay the tax, without being ſued for it; becauſe *it muſt be a poor Heaven indeed that is not worth threepence*—But now we have got a Rector, an *honeſt man*, who lives amongſt us (except when he goes to the mill a grinding, and then he is not far off) a man, who never exacts the *full tenth* of our crop or cattle, but takes from a *fair farmer*, almoſt what he likes to give, ſpends what he takes amongſt his neighbours, for the modeſt and frugal ſupport of his family, and gives the overplus to the relief of the *worthy poor*—I pay my tithe (d'ye mind) to *him* every year with pleaſure—When I hired my farm (obſerve ye) I knew it was ſubject to tithes—had it been tithe free, I muſt have paid much more rent for it than I now do—my Landlord (obſerve ye) would have taken what my Rector now takes, and although I like my Landlord much, I reſpect my Rector more, and, therefore, as I hired my farm (obſerve ye) with my eyes open, and ſaw clear enough it was ſubject to tenths or tithes, were I to withhold them from our worthy Rector, I ſhould think myſelf a *thief* and a *robber.*

Quaker—

Quaker—I efteem thy Rector perhaps more than thou doft, but tithe-taking is his bread —I could wifh he would live and ferve in the tabernacle freely—" freely thou haft received and freely give," faid our Mafter.

Hodge—Pray Mifter Quaker, have you not Parfons, or holders-forth amongft you?

Quaker—Yea.

Hodge—What have they for their preachments?

Quaker—Nothing, kindneffes of the Society excepted, unlefs they travel. When our public friends travel, our private friends receive them, and for the fake of their *living testimony*, they are provided with provinder, carriages, &c. and are borne free from place to place till their return—mean-time their families at home are employed in honeft trades, or callings to fupport themfelves—if they be not able to do fo, our friends are always ready to adminifter to the induftrious members, and make their fituation tolerable, perhaps rather comfortable, 'till the head of the family has cleared himfelf of his Teftimony, and having done his duty, returns home in peace.

Hodge—

Hodge—Hark ye! It comes all to a reckoning with the cafe of our Rector, he employs (obferve ye) all his time in doing good, his dame fpends hers in making fhirts, fhifts, caps, handkerchiefs, and other things for the poor. His two girls too knit ftockings and give them away to ftockinglefs children— The only fault the Rector has, is coming here a grinding—there he puzzles me, for he will have it (his own way) and fay, with the Doctor and the reft at the mill, that a man can never be happy unlefs he be ground down, and pafs through all the operations of this new-fangled mill—I know not what to think, there have been times when I thought of being ground myfelf, and I came here to day with the thought in my head, but meeting with you here, *a Quaker*, put me rather out of temper, and, d'ye mind, I think I muft e'en give up the matter of grinding.

Quaker—I will plainly tell thee, friend, thou never canft be happy till ground young, but, look yonder; there are fome people approaching the mill, one of them, by his black garb I fufpect to be an hireling; if thou wilt walk with me into this meadow

(of

(of contemplation) thou wilt foon become thoughtful, and I feel a defire to have further communications with thee on ferious fubjects.

. *Hodge*—Well, (obferve ye) you feem civil, I will e'en walk with you.

Hodge and the friend walked into the meadow for farther converfation, where we'll leave them for a while, and clofe the 10th Chapter, in order that in

CHAPTER XI.

We may fee who the feveral perfons are that the friend perceived were approaching the mill.

CHAPTER

CHAPTER XI.

Their characters explained, and they prove to be a Popish Priest—A Presbyterian—A Baptist—A Methodist Preacher—And a New Jerusalemite, with parcels of their respective flocks—The professors weighed—Some found wanting, &c.

THOSE who marched at the front were a Papist, a Presbyterian, a Baptist, a Methodist Preacher, and a disciple of Emmanuel Swedenbourg, usually called a teacher of the church, stiled the New Jerusalem; each had a select number of disciples who followed their respective Pastors in the rear, and they all, with steady steps, came up to the mill, professing esteem and friendship for the people there, averring, they had every one of them passed through the operations, and signifying, that by long experience they had obtained the knowledge of several *improvements in grinding*, which they were free to communicate to all, but especially to any candidate for youth and happiness, who should

casually

cafually come, during their ftay, to pafs
through the mill-works—The Rector, Doctor, young men, and all at the mill, received
them cordially—and foon fpread the table
with wholefome refrefhments, of which they
all betook temperately (a few excepted) after which it was propofed to take a view of
the works and wards; in paffing the ward
of *Trial*, fome of the forwardeft and moft
confident of each church or fect, feeing the
fcales, propofed to prove their ponderoufnefs,
and refolved to be weighed—others, more fear-
ful and lowly, wifhed to weigh, but trembled
as they came up to the fcales.

The Rector gently ftepped up to a nimble
profeffor (who was *felf-placed* in the fcale ;
and who, finding it eafily go down with
him, exclaimed, fee here, friends, here's a
full down fcale in me) and the faid Rector
putting the ftandard weights in the oppofite
fcale, rather haftily, up flew the other fcale,
in which the profeffor was, and down fell
the boafter; feveral others were weighed, and
much the fame lightnefs was found in them ;
the Doctor, therefore, turned their faces towards the left-hand wall, on which was
written in facred characters,

TEKEL

TEKEL,

(Which being tranflated, fignifies)
" Thou art weighed in the balance, and art
found wanting."

Whereas, feveral others of each fort, who
reluctantly, and with fear entered the Ward
of Trial and Scales of Truth, were weighed
againft Faith, Love, Hope, Patience, Purity,
Charity, &c. &c. and were found, *not
wanting*.

The light, lean, windy, air-bubbled pre-
tenders, were advifed to go through the operations of the mill, and begin with their
firft works; to wit, the Pedeftal, or ftool,
and Ward of Oratory—Some faid they were
fure and certain they had been through the
whole long fince, that they were *good weight
once*, and if once good weight, their *folids*
could never *finally fall away*—that they fuppofed the Rector, or fome of the people at
the mill, had added to the ftandard weights
to deprefs and deceive them, and, therefore,
they would diffent from their mode of weigh-
ing, ftand upon their prefent ftate, and defy
all bigoted deceivers—The Rector advancing
faid to them, Conceited men, you deceive
yourfelves—you expect to attain the end with-

out

out the means; they grew offended, and went away railing—others refolved to go through all the works of the mill till they were ground right young, or to perifh on the fpot—they perfevered, they did go through and became young like " little children."

Our readers may remember we left the Quaker and Hodge walking in the meadow, it is time to fay what was the fubftance and confequence of their well-timed conference.

When Hodge ferioufly confented to walk in the meadow with his new acquaintance the Quaker, he appeared at firft to keep aloof, and directed his fteps to the River of Reafon, out of which he had drank large draughts of good water before—The Quaker had taken in as much of the fame liquid, but, he alfo had been frequently to the *Rivulet*, which he carefully pointed out to his comrade— Hodge was prevailed upon to tafte this fupe- rior water—he tafted and tafted again, at length he was fo delighted with the fpirit of that peculiar water, that he afked for and had a large draught thereof; fo foon as he felt the falutary and fpeedy effects, and took another turn or two in the meadow of con- templation—he began to cry out, What is
the

the matter with my eyes? I fee things dif-
ferently to what I ever did—I fee, I have
fpent my time and labour chiefly in *vanity*.
And I find now vexation of fpirit—What
have I been doing all thefe laft 40 years?
Why drudging after the world—labouring
to get hread and fupport my family with
the character of an *honeft man*, but I never
was an *happy man*; I now fee I want to know
others *much*—to know myfelf *more* and *moft*
of all, to know from whom I had my being
—Good Quaker, forgive my foftnefs—you
fee Hodge unhodge himfelf—I begin to like
you, though at firft onfet I derided you,
now I fee clearly, you are a far better man
than ever I was—the fight of my paft pur-
fuits and follies fright me—Hodge is grown
old, and as (you fee) almoft crippled with
labour—Hodge cannot be long in this world
—he has been told of a world to come, but
knows nothing about it—he has all religion
to feek, except the name of it; what fhall I
do? where fhall I fly?—I have heard of a
place of torment (I now remember it) for
them that *forget God*—I have too long forgot
him—forboding fears fuggeft I fhall furely be
loft; tell me, Quaker, tell me if you can,

whether

whether it be poffible for an old grey-headed God-forgetting finner, to flee from the wrath to come?

Quaker—Friend, be ftill, thou art old in years, and perhaps not young in vanity, but there is hope concerning thee in Ifrael—thou mayeft yet be both renewed and reftored; only go through the inward works of this mill.

Hodge—Friendly ftranger, is it poffible? is it poffible to reftore one weakened and grown old as I am? can fuch things be? if they can be indeed, and if they really are, let us go to the mill, forthwith; I will go through any of the works, all the works; be any thing, or do any thing, fo that at the end I may be what I wifh and pant to be; fo that I may become vigorous (or young) and happy—but who will direct me in the operations?

Quaker—Thou art already directed in a mea- fure—let us, as you crave, go to the mill — the *Chief Operator*, whom thou haft not feen with carnal eyes, will direct thee—attend to his inward admonitions, and thou fhalt be led into all truth—The ferious fons of peace at the mill, who are inftruments in the hands

hands of the Great Operator, will give thee
all the affiftance in their power; if thou
wilt accept my feeble efforts in thy favour,
I will attend thee, whilft thou art in the
wards of Trial and Oratory; yea, I will
keep there, and in the Silent Ward, till thou
paffeft through the grinders, and comeft out
of the mill vigorous, and (as it were) young.
Hodge thankfully accepted the Friend's affiftance—they drew near the mill together
—It happened that (Hannah) Hodge's wife,
his daughter Audrey, and fon Robert, (it
being now near fun-fet) were come to the
mill—all the people there, the Rector, Doctor, young men, and others, to wit, the Papift, Prefbyterian, Baptift, Methodift and
New Jerufalemite, feeing Hodge and the
Quaker drawing nigh, came to the door to
view and receive them ; Mrs. Hodge, however, and her children kept behind, fearing
Hodge, on feeing them there, would either
grow humorous or angry—but on their nearer
approach, feeing him with one hand leaning
on the Quaker's arm, and hanging down his
head, whilft with the other he held his
handkerchief up to his face, Hannah could
no longer lag behind, but fearing fome
accident

accident had happened to her hufband, or
that he had been taken ill, fhe exclaimed to
her children, fomething ails your father! and
inftantly running to the mill door, (they
quick behind her) with eager emotion fhe
afked, My dear hufband, what is the matter with you? are you not well?

No, no, Hannah, (fays Hodge) I am far
enough from well, poor Hodge may never
be well again—I am wretched (dear wife)
undone, I doubt, quite undone, but don't
be vexed, I deferve all that has or can befall
me—you my wife, and you my children,
have done your duty, you are happy, I am
miferable, and muft be fo I fear for ever—
Here tears and fighs ftopped the powers of
fpeech—Hannah and the children as yet
ftrangers to the caufe of his grief, all fell
into tears—The Quaker, who had loft hold
of Hodge, for the wife and children now
partly fupported and clung round him, and
had feparated him from his former aid—The
Quaker (I fay) ferioufly exclaimed—Friends,
be ftill, thy hufband, thy father, may do
well—His malady is not without in the flefh,
but within in the fpirit, the inward man—
all will be peace, I truft, anon—but their
united

united cries, before they well underftood the
friend, brought all the affembly at the mill
without the door—each enquired—each
wondered—mean time, Hodge, leaning on
his wife and children, got up the fteps, entered the firft room, and being faint, fat
down foftly on the pedeftal, or ftool, that (as
was faid before) ftood there juft at the entrance.

Here, he fent forth fuch a flood of tears,
and vented fuch vehement exclamations againft
himfelf and his former courfe of life, that
many at the mill thought it neceffary to
draw him off the pedeftal, others thought
it more proper to let him remain there a due
feafon; the laft advifers formed a clear
majority, and amongft them were the Rector
and Doctor, Hannah his wife, his fon and
daughter, the Methodift Preacher, &c.—
The Quaker had, before this, retired firft
into the Oratorial Ward, then into the Silent Ward—Hodge at length cried aloud,
give me fomething to comfort me or I muft
faint—The Rector fetched a little excellent
wine, the Doctor flew to the medical cheft,
he brought a bottle of the very beft fal vo-
latile,

latile, and another of lavender drops, mixed
with spirits peculiar to the place; Hannah
had a sprig of myrrh about her; Robert a
rose, and Audrey an apple, plucked off an
apple tree amongst the trees of the wood; all
brought them to the weeping farmer; he
tasted of the wine, took some of the drops,
received the sweet odour of the rose, tasted
of the apple, and all, but especially the last,
refreshed him—He became a little composed
for the present, but soon feeling his sorrow
afresh, he broke out again into deep lamenta-
tions—all the people at the mill were soon in
profound consultation about him, all wished
him well, and all strove to console him—
the Catholic, or Popish Priest, first pushed
himself forward, and addressed the company
after the following Romish fashion:—

Catholic—Gentlemen, schism, as you will
soon know, is a most dangerous and dreadful
thing—you have an instance before your
faces, in the unhappy person on the pedestal
—to be out of the pale of the church is to
be out of the way of salvation—This farmer
(Hodge) owns he has " done the things he
ought not to have done, and has left undone

done the things he ought to have done,"
there is no health in him (you all know or
confefs the fame things, and yet you refufe
to return and lean upon the bofom of our
holy father, the Pope of Rome)—this farmer is bound by the chains and fetters of his
fins, grown grey in error, and fo funk in
forrow, that all of you together cannot deliver him; your mill itfelf is of no ufe except
fo far as you have followed the Catholic
model and manner of working—now, here
am I, ready to help this man of woe, by
the authority I have received from Saint Peter's fucceffor, and by virtue of my facred
function, I have power to releafe him; only
withdraw, leave the man to me, and if he
will frankly confefs and repeat a few Ave
Marias and Pater Nofters, I will forgive him
all that he hath done amifs, and ftake my
welfare againft his that he fhall be whole,
and come off founder and better than any
one ever did, who have adopted your way of
grinding.

Prefbyterian—Father Friar, you have no
more power to reftore him, than you had to
create him.

All

All—Very true—very true.

Baptift—It may be of the utmoft confequence to plunge him forthwith in yonder capacious bath.

Rector—He has not been immerfed, but he was fprinkled when an infant.

Papift—The Bath do little good either to young or old, till the waters are mixed with holy fpittle and falt.

Methodift—If thefe forrows end rightly as I believe they will, he fhall have peace and joy, fuch as none of us can give him.

The Quaker who before this came from the filent ward and joined them, faid:

Quaker—Job, when furrounded with erroneous friends, dealt plainly with them, and affirmed, they were miferable comforters—Phyficians of no value—fuch are fome of you, let him alone, the guide that hath led him thus far, will conduct him through all the needful operations of the mill, and lead him to true peace.

Methodift Preacher—The worthy Friend is in the right—leave the farmer, let him alone.

Young Men, &c.—Let him read the records of the mill.

Papift:—

Papift—They will not d `—let him, by way of preface, read the Pope's bulls and traditions of the Holy Fathers.

Jerufalemite—Your records are of no great ufe, your mill of lefs, and your bulls and traditions of none at all—let him read the works of *Emmanuel Swedenbourg*, who has converfed not only with the inhabitants of the planetary and other worlds, but alfo with Angels and Heavenly fpirits; reading thofe works will lead him to a walk in a delightful field, he will become as brifk as a youth of 25, and not only feel himfelf young and airy, but by the New Jerufalem lanthorn he will fee through all your ways of darknefs, and penetrate the regions of the after-world —he will fee the ftreets of our New Jerufalem, fee the houfes and inhabitants of the future ftate, and, perhaps, get a glance at the very tenement he fhall dwell in, and the lands he fhall till and fow, if he turns out a farmer in that celeftial country.

Rector—The records of our mill fpeak of an *Emmanuel* infinitely greater and more glorious than your German author—though he might be a well-meaning religious man— and they fpeak alfo of a future city, not built

upon.

upon airy imaginations, for that city hath foundations—I ſhall in due time adviſe my reſpected neighbour to ſearch the ſacred records, but, at preſent, I humbly conceive it will be beſt to remove the farmer, if he thinks proper, to the *Oratorial Ward*, and leave him there alone.—To this neceſſary movement, a univerſal conſent was then given—but before Hodge aroſe, Robert, Hodge's ſon, (a brilliant youth) came forward, and thus addreſſed the whole aſſembly of paſtors.

Fathers and reverend paſtors—your opinions are as different as your garments, they are wide and various; your voices, in diſputable points, form a ſort of *Polyglot*; your languages being confounded, prove to demonſtration, you have all, more or leſs, been at the Tower of Babel; but ſuffer me to aſk, do you acknowledge, one and all, that when a man is become old or unhappy by omitting to do right, or doing wrong, he cannot afterwards be made young or happy unleſs he be ground or renewed?—the operations, or modes of grinding may differ, but do you unanimouſly agree, that all muſt paſs through them, and be prepared for a place where per-

petual

petual fummer and perpetual youth are found, or that the long wifhed-for city cannot be entered ?

One and all allowed it to be fo, except the Catholic, who affirmed there is a purgatorial mill that lies between this place and, that city, where, if people are not ground clean here, they may be ground in the hot mill, and drofs-dreffed there; and in due time, by the help of good Catholical petitions (and fo forth) be admitted into the wifhed-for garner.

But that doctrine being over-ruled and borne down by all the reft, the Farmer, who had fat forrowful, yet very attentive, and had heard the whole difputation, lifted up his head, he looked for his wife and children, for the Quaker and Methodift Preacher, for the young men at the mill, and for all he knew, and humbly requefted, that he might not be farther troubled with vain janglings; if there is a way to vigour, faid he, fhew me that way, I am not a good walker now, if I was, I know of no other mill than this—here on this ftool I have opened my mind, I have cloaked nothing, fhew me the way, therefore, to what you call the Ward Oratorial.

The

The Rector and Doctor took Hodge by his hands, they led him forward, his wife and children followed him, the Quaker would not leave him, the Methodist kept close to him, all the rest wished to attend him, and every one entered with him into the Oratorial Ward—Hodge felt a fervour soon as he entered the sacred place, he inftantly became an orator; he spoke in a new ftyle, and with such a peculiar fervour, as his wife or children had never heard before, in short, he lifted up his voice so loud, and spoke so long, that the Rector, fearing he should be exhaufted, opened the *window* that fronted the Chief Mount—Hodge arofe, and going to the cafement for air, difcovered, at a small distance, *a wonderful spectacle*, which aftonished and comforted him, it was the appearance of *one* who bore a heavy load, a burthen which Hodge believed was his own; and when he saw him sink under it, rife again, and throw it like a millftone into the neighbouring sea (never to rife more) he exclaimed—That is my friend, my fubftitute, and my Saviour!

The watchful Rector inftantly brought Hodge the records of the mill, and defired, after taking fome refrefhment, he would look them over; Hodge replied, I am refrefhed, pleafe to leave me here by myfelf, I will perufe the records and fee (for my eyes are better than they were) what thefe records contain—The Rector and the reft left him in the Ward of Oratory—Hodge began at the firft leaf, and perfevered, till he deliberately read through the whole—There he learned to know the glorious great *Father* who made all things—the moft merciful *Son* of the Father (the fame he faw bearing his burthen, who redeemed the fin-fold fons of men)—the *Chief Operator**, who leads and comforts all thofe who follow his directions —and there he faw the moft inimitable drawings (not only of the mill itfelf and all its real works, but alfo) ftriking pictures of the creation of our world, the formation of man and his helpmate, their fall, their firft promife from the Creator, their covering of fkins made of the beaft flain to cloath them, their banifhment, their confequential toil and doom—" Thou fhalt earn thy bread by the fweat of thy brow;"—Ah, true, fays Hodge, I

* The Holy Ghoft.

have

have earned my bread fo from a boy till now
—" Duft thou art, and unto duft fhalt thou
return"—(I know it, I know it, fays he;
but I have a part not made of duft, it will
return to my father, I am his offspring). He
read alfo the encreafe and wickednefs of the
antidiluvian world—the flood—Ay, ay, fays
he, we have turned upon my farm, far from
the fea, fifh bones, fifhes fhells, and other
matters, all proofs of that flood—He read
the ftory and faw the picture of the ark—a
painting of Noah met his eye, ditto of his
wife, of his family, the raven, the dove, and
the reft of the ark on the mountain called
Arrarat—he next viewed the encreafe of the
human fpecies from eight perfons, Noah's
defect, his fon's behaviour, Abraham's call,
his life, the promife made to him, his con-
nexion by his wife, Sarah's defire with
Agar, her fon, her and his banifhment,
Ifaac's birth, his marriage with Rebecca,
their fons Jacob and Efau's wonderful ftory,
the hiftory of Jacob's fons, Jofeph's remarkable life, the treachery of his Brethren, his
faithfulnefs and advancement in Egypt, the
particulars of the Patriarchs, their feveral
prophetical allotments, the captivity of

Abraham's

Abraham's feed; the birth, choice, and
works of Mofes; the wonderful plagues of
Egypt, Pharaoh's obftinacy, the deftruction
of him and all his hoft in the Red Sea, Ifrael's moft wonderful walk through the waters; the life and adminiftration, the view
from Pefgah, and death of Mofes; the fall
of the Ifraelites in the wildernefs, the wars
and victories of Jofhua at the head of their
children, the divifion of the Promifed Land,
the prophecies of the Prophets; the coming
of the *Meffiah*, his birth, life, doctrine, fuf-
ferings, death, refurrection, and afcenfion;
the calling, lives, travels, and fuccefs of the
Apoftles; the rife and progrefs of the firft
(fpiritual *mills* or) *churches*; the doctrine of
Chrift in the four gofpels; the *wide gate* and
broad road which terminate in a gulph of
endlefs mifery; the *ftraight gate* and narrow
way, which lead to life eternal; the lives and
works, the fuccefs and death of the Apoftles; their fundry epiftles to the ancient
churches, and the wonderful revelations
of St. John the Divine.

These things fo inftructed, encouraged and
charmed Hodge, that he refolved to go

Q.   through

through every operation, fo that he might become *like a little child*, young again here; and be affured of the happinefs hereafter, which all, who are truly ground down and renewed, will certainly receive.

He had no fooner declared his refolution, than certain people, who juft arrived to take a view of the mill, and who, after feeing the works, affirmed, fome of them were un- neceffary, came into the ward were Hodge was, and after hearing his cafe, they pro- tefted *he was ground enough already*—for, faid they, he has been on the ftool (as we fee) and have been made forrowful, he will never, we hope, go the old ways again—and hav- ing feen the Mount, and Him who bore his load, throw it into the fea, he has no more to do, but to cheer up, hold faft what he then believed, and conform to our *orders*, in which, if he walks as we fhall direct him, by reading the records, coming conftantly to the mill, reforting to the Oratorial Ward, and, at fet times *fupping* with the mill-men, there can be no doubt whatever, but he will be as young as the beft of them.

The *Papift* encountered their affertions— he proclaimed aloud, that Hodge could ne-

ver

ver become right again till he returned to the *mother church*.

The *Baptiſt* ſaid, he would not be altogether what he ought to be till he was buried for a moment in the bath—This brought on a diſputation, in which the Baptiſt had the better of the argument, though the ſincere *Quaker* ſaid truly, and the *Methodiſt* confirmed the ſaying, there was *a better way of waſhing the inner man*, which they hoped Hodge would inwardly attend to.

The Rector ſaid, Hodge had been in the bath, or had been ſprinkled with its waters many years ago.

The diſciple of Swedenbourg warmly proteſted Hodge could never be young again till he joined the *Jeruſalem Church*; for that all the reſt were as wrong as their enemies could wiſh them to be—The Rector, Doctor, young men at the mill, the Methodiſt Preacher, and the friendly Quaker, all inſiſted upon it that Hodge was not ſufficiently ground; and they all united to beſeech him not to *fall ſhort*, but to go through all the other needful works, till he felt himſelf young and vigorous—Hannah, Robert, and Audrey (his wife and children) earneſtly

entreated

entreated him to submit, and pass through, and they also brought the records of the mill to prove farther operations were necessary. What is rather singular, those at the mill formed (but no where else could they make) a clear *majority*—Hodge, who for a time, (till tired) was all attention, heard the arguments, and judged, as well as he could, of the merits of the debate ; after a little pause spoke for himself—

Hear me, my good friends, I am the person chiefly interested in your consultations and debates—I have (in part) attended to what you have all said, *pro* and *con*, and I have called in, after my ears, my eyes, and my own experience, to distinguish what is truth—*Experience*, 'tis truly said, teaches knowledge—I have not much yet, but I have sufficient to let me know, though I have here received unspeakable benefit, I still want more—it is true, my eyes have been enlightened—I have sat on that stool, have opened my heart to him that knows it, I have looked out of yon window. to the mount, and shall never (I hope) as long as I live forget Him I saw there, I feel too an hope I never knew before ; but, after all

this

this, I think myfelf as yet neither perfectly
clean nor fufficiently young—even whilft
you have been difputing, I became fo drowfy,
that I flipped off my feat, and falling upon
fome of the dirt your feet brought into the
room, I have fullied my coat, and dirtied my
linen; *bring me a brufh*, that if the dirt be
dry it may be rubbed off, and I truft to take
care not again to be *talked afleep*—I want
more ftrength and better covering than at
prefent I wear, and I will go through any
thing, every thing that is ordered for fuch
as me, but I will obtain them—let me go
forward—friendly Rector and all friends point
out the way in which I ought further to go.

CHAPTER

CHAPTER XII.

*Hodge consents to be ground—enters the mill
and the works—is drawn aside by his old
companions for a time—joins them to ring a
peal of bob-majors—is alarmed—leaves off
ringing and returns to the mill—is rightly
ground, i. e. made new, and all ends happily.*

HODGE was now conducted to the
Watch Ward, which had for its top a
lofty tower; he entered the ward alone, and
found, for a time, peace there; but after a
while, his peace, in part, was interrupted
by Will. Witty, Farmer Favour-fields, Mr.
Try-lands, and fundry others his old ac-
quaintances, who miffing their *Sunday* pipes
and pots of ftingo at Hodge's farm-houfe,
and alfo hearing that the caufe of the Farmer's difcontinuance of fuch a good old cuftom was entirely to be imputed to his being
at the mill, came in a body to the fpot, and
earneftly requefted to fee and fpeak to him.

The

The Rector, Doctor, Methodist, Quaker,
and people at the mill faid, their friend,
Mr. Hodge, was in a way of doing well;
that he was placed in the *Watch Ward*, and
moſt likely would not wiſh to admit company; but as they at length infifted upon
ſpeaking to him, they where ſhewn to the
outſide of the ward, where they bawled
aloud—Maſter Hodge! good neighbour
Hodge, where are you?—I am here, replied
Hodge—Who are you? and what is your
buſineſs with me?

Anſwer—Who are we?—why ſure you
know our voices, we are your old neighbours and cloſe friends Will. Witty, Tom.
Trylands, and Frank Favour-fields—we have
all been at a loſs about you theſe three weeks
—we have loſt the pleaſure of ſpending our
Sundays at your farm-houſe; and ſo we have
agreed upon a Sunday club at our own
houſes, by turns—we are come to invite
you to join us, and come away from the mill,
or your brains will be turned, and you'll be
ruined—meet us to-morrow, for it is Sunday, and a good day a good deed you know,
befide we ſhan't neglect work; and we ſhall
have at Mr. Witty's the beſt Virginia to-
bacco,

bacco, and some pots of good ale—moreover 'tis gunpowder treason, and we intend to raise the bells, and ring a round peal of merry *bob-majors*, but we cannot do without you, because 'tis you that always call the peal—we have another thing on foot too —the Lords of the Manors, and all our Landlords, are to meet the next day about *enclosing our commons*, and *building a workhouse*; and, as they say, this will be vastly to our advantage, we wish you to join us in such profitable doings.

Hodge heard and felt all they said—and after a pause, he went up to the top of the Watch Ward tower, and addressed his former companions in the following manner:

Old companions or associates, I am at present otherways engaged, I have several operations yet to pass through before the good end I came for can be obtained—I want my strength to be renewed, and to experience something like the vigour of youth; but when those things happen, I shall not join you again in *Lord's-day frolicks*—no more Sunday stingo at my farm—as to a peal on the bells on a *working day*, why, ringing is (as they say) my *hobby-horse*—I feel an inclination

clination to call the bobs, but at prefent, I
dare not venture—As to *enclofing the commons* and *building a workhoufe,* I fhould neither meddle nor make, if the poor would
not be hurt by them, but if I get ftrong
enough I fhall do my beft to oppofe *both* the
meafures—the poor have little left but
common grafs, common ling, furze, flags,
and common liberty; and to cut up all thefe
by the roots at two ftrokes, i. e. (*inclofures,*
and a confequent *workhoufe*) is a tafk that
ought to make the boldeft and moft powerful
adventurer fhudder.

Companions—Well, neighbour Hodge, you
fhall do as you pleafe if you will but make
one of us; we will vote, and ring, and
drink, and do every thing as you bid us, if
you will but come—Now, as to the ringing
bout, we'll put it off till Monday, if you
promife to come and twirl the treble, only
oblige us—Will you come?

Pray, fays Hodge, go your ways, I wifh
you all well—but let me confider of the
affair.

They withdrew, and left him to turn the
matter over.

R   He

He did fo, and walked *out the Watch Ward,*
unknown to any, to confider of this thing—
Enclofing our commons, thought Hodge,
and building a workhoufe, will totally ruin
our poor; as for ringing a peal for gunpowder treafon, there can be but little harm in
that; the confequence was, that on the fixed
day, Hodge wandered from the mill—The
Rector, Doctor, and all the people there
who knew of his intended excurfion, would
fain have perfuaded him not to venture, but,
as they ufe *no force,* he prevailed, and faid,
he was going upon a good caufe, and, therefore, could catch no harm—He did go, and
by his ftrong arguments in favour of the
poor, whom he infifted were already deprived
of almoft every privilege; by his affirming,
if they were drove to defperation, by taking
away commons and rearing up workhoufes,
alias prifons, they might in time (through
repeated provocations) grow fo untoward, as
to oppofe their oppofers, and by fundry other
efforts, the *enclofure and workhoufe plans* were
over-ruled by a great majority—that fo elated
him and thofe that voted on the fame fide
the queftion, that he was eafily prevailed
upon

upon to go with them to the belfry to ring
a peal of *bob-majors*; and, faid they, if it
was not the day next the gun-powder treafon,
we ought to raife the bells, and ring for joy,
that the commons will remain, and that
the workhoufe fcheme is laid afide; in fhort,
Hodge went with them, took the treble,
the bells were raifed, 1, 2, 3, 4, 5, 6, 7, 8;
they were twirled for a time merrily round,
but ferious thoughts began fo to work on
Hodge's mind, that foon after the changes
began, when it became his duty to call the
peal, he was fo harraffed and abfent, that he
began to blunder, and before bobbing time,
called out to the oppofite ringer who pulled
the tenor, and whofe name was Robert Ro-
per—Bob! Bob!—You are wrong faid Robert—I think the fteeple cracks, cried Hodge
—Bob! Bob!—Confufion foon enfued, every
man, but Hodge, ftayed his bell, though
irregularly; but Hodge could not fet up the
treble on her ftays—he let the rope go,
therefore, and the report of ting! ting!—
ting! ting!—ting! ting! ting!—ting! ting!
—ting! till fhe ceafed, caufed the inhabitants of the town to furmife (the clappers
beating out of courfe) that the ropes had

broke,

broke, or that some misfortune had happened
to the ringers—Poor Hodge, however, after
a short and broken apology, saying he dare
ring no more, put on his coat, wished them
well, and sneaked away to the mill again,
sad and sorrowful.

On his return, he was readily received, he
frankly told them how he fared, ran hastily
into the *Oratorial Ward*, and began to cry
out bitterly; being, however, soon calmed,
he resolved afresh to go through all the
works, was removed to the *Fasting Ward*,
there he continued from morning till near
evening, before he took outward refreshment;
after a small repast, the main wheel being
then in full motion, as the water was plen-
tiful, Hodge, unasked, descended into the
hopper, but being soon laid hold of by the
grinders, most vehemently whirled over and
over, and hard pressed between them, he began to be alarmed—fear seized him, that he
should never get through, but perish—the
more so, as in that state of violent agitation
he could scarce see light; the fear of destruc-
tion, and the hope of deliverance, never before appeared so conspicuous; at length his
hope was crowned—he dropped down to
the

the fpout, and came out whole; but his old
garments were ground away, he was nearly
naked, and thought within himfelf, as he
afterwards affirmed, he felt the grinding
powers *within-fide*, as well as *without*; the
people at the mill, ever watchful, rejoiced
at the operations—clean linen were foon
pointed out, decent under-garments appeared, and an *outward robe* to go over all was
given him, fuch as few will wear—Hodge
looked at himfelf, walked like a little child
—anon he leaped, fkipped, and proclaimed,
" *if ever an old man was ground young, I am.*"
He then was led to the Rivulet and drank
more of its fweet ftreams—he was fhewn to
the Ward of Trial, a very warm ward;
Hodge at one time began to fear the fire
would confume him, but an unfeen hand
placed a mill-*fkreen*, between the flame and
him, fo that he fweetly enjoyed the fhade,
till he paffed and was put into the *fcale*—
wherein being fairly poifed as ufual, all the
fpectators pronounced he was *full weight*—
Hodge then embraced them, gave thanks to
the *Chief Operator* afrefh, returned to his
family in peace, and from that day to this,
they have lived together in that harmony and
happinefs

happinefs that none can poffibly experience but fuch as are ground young.

No one rejoiced more at Hodge's converfion than the Methodift Preacher and the pious *Quaker*; at the Quaker's departure he fhook Hodge heartily by the hand, faying, keep clofe to the inward guidance, and good things thou haft received.

The worthy Friend next addreffed himfelf to all the people at the mill, efpecially to the Methodift, who had gained his higheft efteem, faying, Friends, I find that 1 muft foon leave you all; I came here, not only to fee you again face to face and commune with you, but alfo to leave behind a token of love for the fake of the *Chief Operator*, and to you; he then pulled out from his bofom, and gave into the hands of the Rector, Doctor, and Methodift, a large parchment (fealed) fcroll, in which he had made over, for the benefit of the people at the mill, a tract of fertile land lying not far off—the reft of his patrimony he bequeathed to his neareft kindred; and after a fincere and hearty farewell, he left them, and foon after departed this life in peace and in a good old age, leaving behind him an irreproachable character,

racter and many weeping friends; amongst them were numerous poor, to whom in his life time he was a conftant and bountiful benefactor—all to this day bewail his lofs.

The *good Quaker* died a widower, but he left behind him two children; he had many years before well provided for the eldeft, and therefore left him no more than his blefling, and a token of parental love—After feveral fpecific legacies to the poor, he left the refidue of fortune to his youngeft fon—But foon after his remains were entombed (by his own defire, under the flag of a fpot, walled round for the like purpofe, being part of the land he had left to the mill) *Mr. Quirks,* the lawyer, hearing what he made over to the mill, pofted away (his Clerk *Trimmer,* with a paper bag at his heels) to his *eldeft* fon, and thus addreffed him.

Quirks—Good morrow, worthy Sir, I have broke through ten engagements of confequence to attend you to day—I have bufinefs of the utmoft importance, and joyful news indeed to tell you.

Son—What news, Mr. Quirks?

Quirks—News that will tickle your very heart-ftrings, Sir; why I fhall give you to know,

know, Sir, that your father who is dead, has
left you only a trifle—your youngeſt brother
has got what the teſtator choſe to ſpare; but
he has left to the paltry people at yonder mill,
a large parcel of land, contrary to the cuſtom
of the country; and, therefore, I am very
confident (I am ſure on't) that I can take
away the ſaid land from them, and get it for
you—I have now *another* laudable *cauſe* in
hand exactly in point, and am ſure and certain I ſhall recover in the ſame way a conſiderable funded property in the courſe of a few
days.

Son—Your application is ſo unexpected,
Sir, I am not perfectly prepared to anſwer
you—but pray will not the matter, if liti-
gated, be attended with conſiderable expence?

Quirks—Oh, Sir, as to that, why, it may,
to be ſure, coſt a trifle, but don't let the
coſts fright you; I am ſo confident of ſuc-
ceſs, that if you pleaſe (to uſe a phraſe I
often uſe) I will go ſnacks with you, win or
loſe; if we win, as we certainly ſhall, give
me one-half, take you the other; mean time
I have to beg the loan of a few pounds to
pay my agent, and ſo forth.

Son—

Son—Well, but hear me, Mr. Quirks, pray was the land my father's fole property?

Quirks—My dear Sir, no doubt in the world but it was—I can prove whom he bought it of; my Clerk here, Mr. *Trimmer*, has in my bag a copy of the conveyance fixty years ago, from Francis Fullpaid, Efq. to your late deceafed father and his heirs, in fee fimple.

Son—Well, but will it be *honeſt* think you to wreſt it from the mill?

Quirks—Honeſt! aye, Sir, perfectly honeſt, indifputably honeſt; for whatfoever is the cuſtom of the country, of courfe muſt be honeſt.

Son—Hem!—it is not the cuſtom of the country to banifh *all Quirks* from their native land—fuppofe it was, (as it has been the cuſtom in fome countries to banifh other profeſſional people) fhould you like it?

Quirks—Dear Sir, your breeding is too good to fuffer you to infult me—I waited upon you to do you a kindnefs—if we differ in opinion, and you do not chufe to give me the job, why then, Sir, I am, Sir, your moſt humble fervant.

Son—

Son—Good bye to you, Mr. Quirks.

They parted—The fon fent for Mr. *Blackſwan*, who foon came, and between them two the following converfation took place:

Son—Mr. Blackſwan, I have had a Gentleman of the Law, one Mr. *Quirks*, with me, who wiſhed me to employ him in a cuſtomary piece of bufineſs; however, I fent for you, becauſe I rather chufe that you ſhould be concerned as my Attorney.

Blackſwan—What may the nature of the bufineſs be, Sir?

Son—You know my father left a parcel of land to the people at the mill—now, Quirks affirms, by the cuſtom of the country, it may be taken away from them, and recovered for me, as I am my father's eldeſt fon and heir at law; and if I muſt have it, I will not have it till you fue for and recover it for me.

Blackſwan—Then, Sir, you will never have it at all, for I will not be concerned in ſuch fort of bufineſs.

Son—I ſhall pay you, Sir, for what you ſhall do, and I thought it was lawyer's bufineſs

finefs to do what their clients defired of them.

Blackfwan—No, no, not if their. defires do not . accord with . confcience—We are *free agents*, not *bond flaves*—I will not take: this in hand, partly for the fake of the mill and . partly for your fake; for if you could get it (and *the event is hazardous*) if you could grafp it, *contrary to your father's dying donation,* it may perhaps breed a *moth* to eat up all you had before.

Son—Sir, I fay, I will have you my Attorney in this caufe, and you fhall do the bufinefs too—but fuffer me* to explain myfelf, for the bufinefs is this; if there be any cuftom in the country to ravifh from the mill-people, what my father gave them; go tell them, *though I was never ground myfelf,* my *honour* will not fuffer me to take or to touch it; go, Mr. Blackfwan, and quickly. prepare at my expence an inftrument to releafe all my real or fuppofed right in this parcel of land, and let them enjoy it freely for ever.

Blackfwan—Honeft Sir, that I'll do with all my heart, nor will I charge a groat for·

doing

doing it. He did draw and engrofs the ra-
tification and confirmation of the Quaker's .
gift to the mill, the fon nobly executed
it, and thus the matter was pleafingly fet-
tled.

The other *cafe in point*, about feven years
after, was concluded; when lo! the client
of Mr. *Quirks*, found the profeffional bills
fo numerous, and *large*, and the remainder
to him fo *fmall*, that he fpurned at the
trifling furplus, and with a difdainful brow,
told *Quirks*—You pettyfogging fellow, did
not you at firft onfet affure me, you fhould
moft certainly recover the whole for me?

Aye, Aye, fays Quirks, I did, and fo I
moft furely fhould have done, had it not
been for *the glorious uncertainty of the
Law—*

However, Sir, fays he, you have got (in
part) your mind, have you not?

No, wretch, replied the Client, nor never fhall, till I fhake off the demerits of this
foul matter, and fee you ftruck off the roll,
or peep through the pillory.

From thenceforth, the Rector, Doctor,
Methodift Preacher, Hodge, and the people

on

on the fpot, continued in peace—Many were
ground effectually, numbers came continually to the place—public prejudices fubfided,
and others, that never came there, hearing
of the falutary effects of grinding, at this
period, join the Editor to fay

SUCCESS to the MILL.

F I N I S.

February 25, 1791.